PRACTICAL
CANDLEBURNING
RITUALS

PRACTICAL

CANDLEBURNING
RITUALS

**SPELLS & RITUALS
FOR EVERY PURPOSE**

RAYMOND BUCKLAND

Llewellyn Publications
Woodbury, Minnesota

FOURTH EDITION, REVISED
Ninth Printing, 2014

Book design by Kimberly Nightingale
Cover design and interior art by Kevin R. Brown
Cover photograph © 2003, Leo Tushaus

Library of Congress Cataloging-in-Publication Data
Buckland, Raymond.
Practical candleburning rituals.
1. Candles and lights—Miscellanea. 2. Occult sciences.
I. Title. II. Series

BF1442.C35B83   1986   133.4'3   86-20915

ISBN 13: 978-0-87542-048-6

ISBN 10: 0-87542-048-6

Llewellyn Publications
A Division of Llewellyn Worldwide Ltd.
2143 Wooddale Drive
Woodbury, MN 55125-2989
www.llewellyn.com
Llewellyn is a registered trademark of Llewellyn Worldwide Ltd.
Printed in the United States of America

Advanced Candle Magic
(Llewellyn, 1996)

*Amazing Secrets of
the Psychic World*
(Parker, 1975) with
Hereward Carrington

Anatomy of the Occult
(Weiser, 1977)

The Book of African Divination
(Inner Traditions,
1992) with Kathleen
Binger

*Buckland's Complete
Book of Witchcraft*
(Llewellyn, 1986,
2002)

*Buckland Gypsies' Domino
Divination Deck*
(Llewellyn, 1995)

Cardinal's Sin
(Llewellyn, 1996)

Cards of Alchemy
(Llewellyn, 2003)

Coin Divination
(Llewellyn, 1999)

Color Magick
(Llewellyn, 1983,
2002)

The Committee
(Llewellyn, 1993)

Doors to Other Worlds
(Llewellyn, 1993)

The Fortune-Telling Book
(Visible Ink Press,
2003)

Gypsy Dream Dictionary
(Llewellyn, 1990,
1998)

Gypsy Witchcraft & Magic
(Llewellyn, 1998)

Here Is the Occult
(HC, 1974)

The Magic of Chant-O-Matics
(Parker, 1978)

Mu Revealed
(Warner Paperback
Library, 1970)
under the pseud-
onym "Tony Earll"

*A Pocket Guide to
the Supernatural*
(Ace, 1969)

CONTENTS

Part Two: Christian Rituals

INTRODUCTION TO THE THIRD EDITION

Practical Candleburning Rituals has been described as "an occult classic." It has certainly been a popular book for over a decade and has now become available in a Spanish language edition. This is the second time it has been enlarged and, hopefully, it will continue its life for many more years to come.

What makes it so popular? I think it is the "earthiness" of it. It is a collection of simple, practical rituals that are a far cry from the highly esoteric, mystical workings associated with the world of High Magick. The rituals here are of, and for, "the people."

The rituals in this book were collected from around the world. Some are relatively new; some have been around for hundreds of years. They cover many aspects of life; many of the basic needs that "the people" have felt at one time or another — good and bad.

And here, perhaps, there should be a word of caution regarding the ethics of magick. In Witchcraft there is the admonition: *"An' it harm none,* do what thou wilt." And it harm none . . . that includes, of course, yourself. Do nothing to harm another and do nothing to harm yourself. This is not a book on Witchcraft; it is a book on magick. What is the difference? Basically, Witchcraft is a religion* while magick is a practice. In other words, anyone can do magick. Consequently they can do it for good or for ill, depending on their own personal ethics.

---

* See *Witchcraft from the Inside* by Raymond Buckland, Llewellyn Publications: St. Paul, 1971.

Since this is not a book on Witchcraft it does include one or two rituals that you would not find in such a book—"To Arouse Jealousy," "To Break Up a Love Affair," "To Win the Love of a Man or a Woman." To win love . . . ? Yes. This is a deceptively innocuous-sounding ritual, yet consider it. When you set out to influence another's feelings for you, are you not interfering with their free will? Would you want someone to interfere with your own free will?

I think that all the rituals in this book need to be here, if for no other reason than historical interest. I would only ask that you choose the right ritual for you with the above words in mind. Bear in mind, also, that what you ask for is what you get. . . so be quite sure that you really want it before you ask! I deal with this aspect more fully in the exciting new section at the back of the book that deals with creative visualization.

Part of the title of this book—perhaps the most important part—is *practical*. All that is in here is practical. Over the past ten years and more I have received letters from people who have successfully performed the rituals. All have praised the fact that they are easy to do; they need no special equipment; and, if done as directed, they work! All you need are a few candles and the *will* to achieve what you desire. The rest is easy. You create your own reality and through candle manipulation you are able to do so in a most precise manner.

Please read the chapter on Preparation very carefully. It is important. It may, perhaps, appear deceptively simple. It is uncomplicated, yes, but the points that are raised are important ones. Read it and follow it.

I hope you enjoy this new, enlarged, edition of *Practical Candleburning Rituals.* Bright blessings.

Raymond Buckland
Virginia, 1982

Today more and more people are turning to the
occult. Tarot cards and the various methods of their
interpretation are frequently the subject of everyday
conversation. Ouija board parties are more numerous now than ever they were in the days before World
War II. The construction of an astrological natal chart
is common knowledge. Whether this acceptance of
what have heretofore been regarded as "way out"
beliefs and practices is due to Dr. Rhine's experiments
and proof of extrasensory perception; to Professor
Otto Rahn's proof of "power" emanating from the
human body; to Dr. Eisenbud's proof of mind over
matter, or other similar experiments and proofs, we
cannot say. But today there is more belief in, and
practicing of, various types of magic than at any other
time in the checkered history of humankind.

Sympathetic magic is based on the principle that
like attracts like. Make a wax or clay model representing a person and, if you work to the prescribed
formula, whatever you do to the figure will actually
happen to the person. Early humans first discov-
ered this twenty-five thousand years ago in Paleo-
lithic times. In those days, to ensure success in
hunting for food humans would model a clay bison
and then "attack" it and "kill" it. They then felt suffi-
ciently empowered to go out and kill the real bison.
Today, many people are finding that they can work this

same type of magic using candles—not to hunt bison, but to solve many of the problems presented by twentieth-century living. By burning different types of candles and manipulating them in various ways they find they can influence people and things.

This book deals with the practice of candle-burning—what candles to burn and when; how to "manipulate" them for the purposes desired. It deals little with the history of the subject for, as its title states, it is a practical book. It is for those who want to be able to *do* things. Simple yet effective, these rituals can be done right in the home with readily available items of no complexity.

Raymond Buckland

PREPARATION

ROOM

However simple a ritual may be, preparation is all-important. If you are going to burn candles, first of all decide *where* you are going to burn them. Let it be somewhere they can remain undisturbed, for many of the rituals must be done over a period of days with the candles unmoved between times. It should also be a place where there will be no risk of fire—an innocent-looking candle burning too close to a filmy curtain or drape can lead to a conflagration and catastrophe!

Choose a room that is quiet, where you don't hear the television or stereo blaring. Perhaps at the back of the house or apartment, away from the sound of traffic. You need a room where you will be able to carry out your rituals without fear of interruption. The basement or the attic of a house is ideal.

ALTAR

You will need something to act as an altar. Almost anything will do—table, chest, box—even the floor itself. But why not do things properly? A little aestheticism never hurt anyone. A small, low coffee table is ideal—preferably about two and a half feet long by two feet wide. Or a card table would do nicely. If you wish, you may cover it with a cloth. This should be white. You will need a number of candleholders. These may be of any type, any material. Try, however, to choose fairly small ones so that when you are using a number of candles at one time the altar is not too cluttered. This is also important sometimes when you need to stand two or more candles close together. With large candleholders it is impossible to get them close, so keep to the smaller, less elaborate type.

INCENSE

Incense is seldom mentioned in connection with candleburning but, to the author's mind, it is extremely important. Incense should always be burned during a ritual. It is a great aid to concentration—establishing the correct peace of mind necessary as a preliminary step. There is of course the original belief concerning incense, that the ascending smoke carries one's prayers upward to the gods. Virtually any incense will suffice, ranging from the little cones sold in nickel-and-dime stores through to the specially mixed types that must be sprinkled on glowing charcoal. Most people will find the cones most convenient. Of the different ones available, the Indian incenses seem generally preferable to the Chinese. The latter seem just a little too sweet and scented.

In the following rituals if a particular incense is called for it will be mentioned. If no special incense is noted, then you may use any type. However, if you cannot obtain the special ones, then make do with what you can get. "Any incense is better than no incense" should be the general rule.

A simple yet effective censer may be constructed by filling a shallow dish, ashtray, or cup with sand. The incense cones may then be stood on the sand, which will absorb any heat and prevent cracking of the vessel or scorching of the altar.

THE PRACTITIONER

There is no need to fast or even to go on a rigid diet before indulging in the practice of candle-burning. You will be far better able to concentrate on what you are doing if you are well fed and comfortable. A symbolic cleansing is usually indulged in before a ritual, however. This consists simply of a bath. It is a dip into a bath of water to which a handful of salt has been added. The water may be of a comfortable temperature—no need for ascetic coldness. It is simply a dip in and a splashing of the water over the body. No need for soaping.

THE CANDLES

The candles may be of any type; it is the color that is important. There was a time when one was strictly admonished to burn only vegetable oil candles or paraffin candles. Never, never was one to burn candles made of animal oil. Today, although this still holds true, you may safely forget it. Few, if any, candles are now made of animal oil and, as stated, the important thing is actually the color.

The most important preparation in the practice of candleburning is the preparation of the candles themselves. They should be "dressed" before they are used. And to be of maximum effectiveness they should be dressed by the practitioner. Dressing is done with oil. There are a number of different candle-anointing oils on the market with little to choose between them. Some of these oils are colored and should therefore only be used on candles of the same color. It is obviously far less expensive to buy an oil that is colorless and can be used on all your candles. If you cannot obtain candle-anointing oil, then you may use regular olive oil.

To dress a candle you anoint it with the oil, rubbing it into the candle from the center toward the end (see illustration, page 5). Always rub in the same direction; from the center out to one end, then from the center out to the other end. While dressing the candle you should be thinking—concentrating—hard on the subject, problem, or question at hand. (See also "Identification," page 8.) Four types of candles

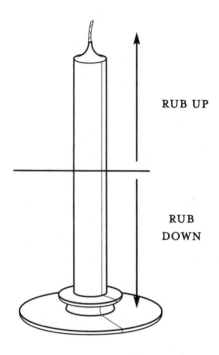

RUB UP

RUB
DOWN

are used in the rituals: altar candles, offertory candles, astral candles, and day candles.

Altar candles—These are two tall white candles that are always on the altar. They are placed at the two far corners and are always lit before any of the others.

Offertory candles—These are the candles in the various symbolic colors (table 3, page 12) dependent upon the work to be done.

Astral candles—These represent the petitioner(s) and are chosen depending on the person's birth date (table 1, page 10). A candle of the primary color may be used or you may purchase astral candles that are made in the two-color combination.

Day candles—These may be used in any of the rituals (table 2, page 11), dependent upon the day of performance. Placed on the right front of the altar.

RITUALS

Rituals are given for all the more frequently dealt-with conditions, plus one or two that are a little out of the ordinary. Two forms of ritual are usually given. One is the customary Christianized form, simplified versions of which are found in the few books currently available on candleburning; the other is a more general traditional form. The latter have been collected by the author from various sources throughout Europe and seem to reflect the early pre-Christian nature worship—the Old Religion as it is known.

Whichever ritual you use will be equally valid. Indeed the finest and most effective words would be spontaneous ones from your heart. Not all of us are able to produce the right words to match our feelings at the right time, however—hence the rituals herein. They need not be learned by heart; they can simply be read from this book. If you make a mistake—don't worry! A small error, a fumble, a slip of the tongue will not negate the ritual. It is the meaning, the purpose within you that is important.

DRESS

Elaborate, ornate robes are not necessary in this practice, unless you feel happier with such trappings. It is largely psychological. The followers of the Old Religion would work naked, as a symbol of freedom. Most people these days wear their ordinary everyday clothes for the rites. But some do feel that a ritual calls for "something special" and consequently wear garments ranging from simple, plain white robes to elaborate, colored silken garments covered with esoteric symbols. If they feel their rituals will be more effective through the use of these "props," more power to them! They are not, however, mandatory.

ALTAR FIGURE

Although it is not necessary to the rituals many people like to include a religious figure or picture in the altar arrangements. A crucifix, an ankh, a figure of Jesus, Mary, or an ancient Venus figurine would be quite permissible. The figure or picture should be placed at the back of the altar in the center, with the censer immediately before it.

LIGHTING AND EXTINGUISHING OF CANDLES

It is best to light a taper and then to light the candles on the altar from this, in the order noted. At the close of the ritual you may blow out the flames—in reverse order to that of lighting—or you may put them out with a candle snuffer. Do not pinch them out with your fingers.

TIME OF RITUALS

Most of the rituals state the days on which they should be performed, or the number of days. The time of day, unless specified, is left to you. Whatever hour gives you greatest ease, be it early morning, midday, or late evening will suffice. But choose a time when you are unlikely to be interrupted.

IDENTIFICATION

It is actually possible to use candles without dressing them, but far more effective to dress them. Table I on page 10 gives the appropriate colors for birth dates—but suppose you don't know the birth date of the person in question? All you do then is use a plain white candle to represent them, concentrating on the person as you dress it.

A FINAL WORD BEFORE STARTING

Rituals are more than just words. They have meaning. Whichever of the following rituals you plan to do first, sit quietly and read it through. Think about the words, their meaning. This way you will not be repeating something "parrot fashion" but will be getting closer to the ideal of using your own words—words from the heart.

Of the two types of rituals given in this book many people favor the Old Religion, or non-Christian, rituals simply because the wordings are so pertinent to the aims of the rituals. In so many of the traditional Christian versions, the words of the psalms used seem to have no bearing whatsoever in the operation. Yet many, many people have had great success whichever version they have used.

Read them, then, and use that which you find most pleasing to *you*. First and foremost you should feel happy and comfortable with what you use.

The book is divided into two parts, part one being the Old Religion version of the rituals, and part two being the Christian version of the rituals. You can use the version you like best, or mix and match.

TABLE I	**Astral Colors**		
ZODIAC SIGN	BIRTH DATE	PRIMARY COLOR	SECONDARY COLOR
Aquarius	Jan. 20–Feb. 18	BLUE	Green
Pisces	Feb. 19–Mar. 20	WHITE	Green
Aries	Mar. 21–Apr. 19	WHITE	Pink
Taurus	Apr. 20–May 20	RED	Yellow
Gemini	May 21–June 21	RED	Blue
Cancer	June 22–July 22	GREEN	Brown
Leo	July 23–Aug 22	RED	Green
Virgo	Aug. 23–Sept. 22	GOLD	Black
Libra	Sept. 23–Oct. 22	BLACK	Blue
Scorpio	Oct. 23–Nov. 21	BROWN	Black
Sagittarius	Nov. 22–Dec. 21	GOLD	Red
Capricorn	Dec. 22–Jan. 19	RED	Brown

TABLE 2   **Days of the Week**

Sunday	Yellow
Monday	White
Tuesday	Red
Wednesday	Purple
Thursday	Blue
Friday	Green
Saturday	Black

TABLE 3   **Symbolism of Colors**

White	Purity, truth, sincerity
Red	Strength, health, vigor, sexual love
Light blue	Tranquility, understanding, patience, health
Dark blue	Impulsiveness, depression, changeability
Green	Finance, fertility, luck
Gold/yellow	Attraction, persuasion, charm, confidence
Brown	Hesitation, uncertainty, neutrality
Pink	Honor, love, morality
Black	Evil, loss, discord, confusion
Purple	Tension, ambition, business progress, power
Silver/gray	Cancellation, neutrality, stalemate
Orange	Encouragement, adaptability, stimulation, attraction
Greenish-yellow	Sickness, cowardice, anger, jealousy, discord

Part One

Old Religion
Rituals

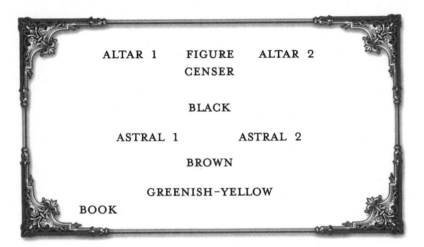

ALTAR 1   FIGURE   ALTAR 2
CENSER

BLACK

ASTRAL 1   ASTRAL 2

BROWN

GREENISH-YELLOW

BOOK

To Break Up a Love Affair

Light altar candles 1 and 2.

Light incense and sit for a moment thinking of the love affair *as it is at present.*

Light astral 1 (the astral candle of the man in the affair) and picture the man, as you say:

Here is the male half of the pair.
He is half of a whole; soon will he be single.

Light astral 2 (the astral candle of the woman in the affair) and picture the woman, as you say:

> *Here is the female—the second half of the pair.*
> *Soon will she too be single.*

Light black candle and say:

> *Here starts discord. Here burneth confusion.*

Light brown candle and say:

> *Uncertainty fills their minds.*
> *They hesitate.*
> *Are they right for one another, they think?*
> *Should they really be together?*
> *. . . doubt fills their minds.*

Light greenish-yellow candle and say:

> *Here be jealousy!*
> *Here be discord!*
> *Here be worries, doubts, anger, and fear.*
> *So shall it work.*

Think now of the couple breaking up. Think of the love affair being over; of them going their separate ways. Say:

> *What was attractive*
> *now seems plain.*
> *What was entertaining*
> *now is boring.*

What was pretty
now is sullied.
What was bright
now is dull.
What drew together
now detracts.
What lived
dies.
No longer the love that flared between them;
no longer the fires of passion flaming;
no longer the longing and the yearning;
no longer the two becoming one.
Dull is their love;
dowsed are the fires;
gone is the longing;
separated are they.

Think again, for a few moments, of the affair being completely over; the two people separated. Then say:

Violets are dead, a faded ribbon,
and a dusty curl or so;
half-torn notes, forgotten tokens
of some heartache long ago.

Kneeling by the hearthstone sadly,
see, I throw them in the grate;
crackling now they burn, these ruins
Of my joys and luckless fate.

Lovers' vows, oaths false and flighty,
up the chimney fast they fly;
and the little god, I fancy,
all unseen, stands chuckling by!

Still I sit beside the hearthstone,
dream—of what I cannot tell;
watch the sparks amid the ashes
dying out.
Goodnight! Farewell!

Extinguish the candles. Repeat this ritual every Saturday evening, each time moving the two astral candles an inch or so further apart. Repeat until they eventually reach the two opposite sides of the altar.

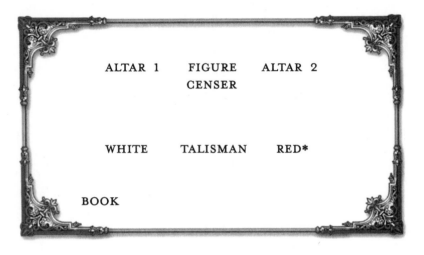

```
        ALTAR 1      FIGURE      ALTAR 2
                     CENSER


        WHITE      TALISMAN      RED*

   BOOK
```

Consecration of an Amulet or Talisman

This ritual is for the consecration of a talisman, an amulet, or a "good luck charm." The talisman may be one that was made for you by someone else, or one that you made yourself. The latter is preferable.

Light altar candles 1 and 2.

Light incense (frankincense recommended).

Light white candle and say:

Here burns the sincerity of . . . (petitioner's name) . . . ,
his/her belief in the power of the talisman burns
as strongly as does this flame.
It will never die.

Light red* candle and say:

Here is the love that goes into the talisman.*
For the talisman is a storehouse
of the power of love.

Take up the talisman and, holding it by the edge, pass it three times through the flame of the white candle, turning it over so that both sides are touched by the flame. (Don't burn your fingers!) Say:

By fire do I cleanse this talisman of any and all impurities
that may dwell within it.

Now pass it three times through the smoke of the incense, saying:

And by the gods I cense and cleanse it to be ready for my purpose.

Now take the talisman and hold it firmly in your right hand (left hand if left-handed) and say:

This talisman I imbue with love.
Whoever shall wear it shall feel that awesome power.
That power will be ever with its wearer,
so long as she/he shall bear it.

---

* The color and purpose of this candle will depend upon the purpose of the talisman (i.e., red for love; blue for health; green for fertility, etc.)

Now pass the talisman three times through the flame of the red candle. Say:

Here is that love, fully consecrated within.

Lay the talisman between the white and red candles. Extinguish the flames.

Let the talisman remain undisturbed for three hours. It should then be carried, or worn, by its owner, preferably worn next to the skin.

BAD HABIT

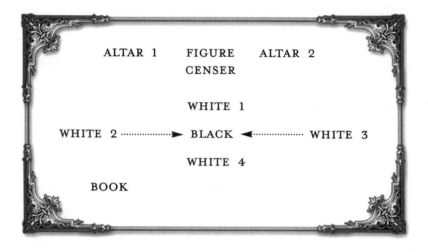

ALTAR 1   FIGURE   ALTAR 2
           CENSER

           WHITE 1

WHITE 2 ··············▶ BLACK ◀·············· WHITE 3

           WHITE 4

    BOOK

To Overcome a Bad Habit

Light altar candles 1 and 2.

Light incense (preferably frankincense) and sit for a moment thinking of the bad habit slowly fading away and being overcome by good.

Light black candle, and say:

> *Here is that which holds me back.*
> *It is not good for me and well do I know it.*

It seems a mighty giant
that is not to be conquered.
Yet do I know that not to be so,
for conquer it I will.

Light white candles 1, 2, 3, and 4 and say:

Here is my strength; here is my courage;
Here is my fortitude; here is my victory.
Now is mine enemy surrounded.
Now knows he not which way to turn.
The battle doth begin,
Yet is the end well known.

Picture in your mind the forces of good advancing, marching on the enemy—the bad habit. After a few moments of this, say quietly:

Star of the twilight gray,
where wast thou blinking?
When in the olden day,
eve dim was sinking?
"O'er knight and baron's hall,
turret, and tower,
o'er fell and forest tall,
green brake and bower."

Star of the silver eve,
what hast thou noted,
while o'er the tower and tree
high hast thou floated?
"Blue blades and bonnet gear,

plaids lightly dancing,
lairs of the dun deer,
and shafts dimly glancing."

Star of the maiden's dream,
star of the gloaming,
where now doth blink thy beam,
when owls are roaming?
"Where in the baron's hall
green moss is creeping,
where o'er the forest's fall
gray dew is weeping."

Star of the even still,
what now doth meet thee,
when from the lonely hill
looks thy blink sweetly?
"Hearths in the wind bleached bare,
roofs in earth smouldered,
sheep on the dun deer's lair,
trees felled and mouldered."

After a few moments more of picturing the bad habit finally overcome, extinguish the candles—black first, then white 4, 3, 2, and 1.

At the same time seven days later, repeat the ritual but first move white candles 2 and 3 an inch in toward the black. Repeat weekly until the two whites touch the black.

CONDITIONS

ALTAR 1   FIGURE   ALTAR 2
              CENSER

PINK

PETITIONER

LIGHT BLUE   ORANGE

BOOK

To Settle a Disturbed Condition in the Home

Light altar candles 1 and 2.

Light incense.

Sit for a moment and meditate, getting clear in your mind just what you want to accomplish.

Light petitioner's candle, thinking hard on the petitioner. Say:

This candle represents . . . (name). . . .
As it burns, so burns his/her spirit.

Light the light blue, pink, and orange candles, in
that order, thinking of peace and tranquility, of understanding and love in the house in question. Then say:

Here burns happiness about . . . (name) . . . ,
it is in his/her house; it is all about him/her.
There is tranquility in the home.
Peace and love abound and are with him/her.
For true happiness now is known.
Understanding and love are there in abundance;
discord and chaos are fled.
For be it ever thus, that as patience and
love do grow and prosper so barren become
the fields of doubt and distress.
Happiness is the light that burns and
darkness all away is sent.
The home is peace; peace is the home.

Sit then for three to five minutes concentrating
on settling the disturbed condition in the home.
Then say again:

Here burns happiness about . . . (name) . . . ,
it is in his/her house; it is all about him/her.
There is tranquility in the home.
Peace and love abound and are with him/her.
For true happiness now is known.
Understanding and love are there in abundance;
discord and chaos are fled.

For be it ever thus, that as patience and
love do grow and prosper so barren become
the fields of doubt and distress.
Happiness is the light that burns and
darkness all away is sent.
The home is peace; peace is the home.

Again sit for three to five minutes concentrating on settling the disturbed condition in the home. Then, for the third time, say:

Here burns happiness about . . . (name) . . . ,
it is in his/her house; it is all about him/her.
There is tranquility in the home.
Peace and love abound and are with him/her.
For true happiness now is known.
Understanding and love are there in abundance;
discord and chaos are fled.
For be it ever thus, that as patience and
love do grow and prosper so barren become
the fields of doubt and distress.
Happiness is the light that burns and
darkness all away is sent.
The home is peace; peace is the home.

Again sit for three to five minutes concentrating on settling the disturbed condition in the home. Then extinguish the candles.

This ritual should be repeated on three consecutive nights.

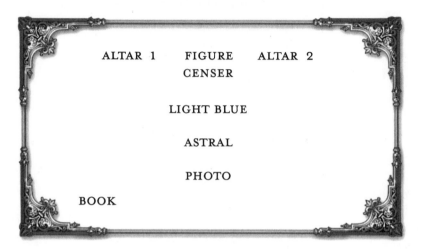

ALTAR 1   FIGURE   ALTAR 2

CENSER

LIGHT BLUE

ASTRAL

PHOTO

BOOK

For the Dead

(*Note:* In this ritual a photograph of the deceased may be placed before his or her astral candle.)

Light altar candles 1 and 2.

Light incense.

Light astral candle of the deceased and picture him or her in your mind as you remember best, preferably on some especially happy occasion. Say:

Here stands. . . . (name) . . .
who will never die.
His/her spirit burns on as does this candle flame.

Light light blue candle and say:

Here is peace and tranquility.
Such is his/hers, now and always.

Then, thinking of the person happy and at peace, say:

To know, to dare, to will, to keep silent;
are the four words of the magus.
In order to dare, we must know;
in order to will, we must dare;
we must will to possess empire;
to reign we must keep silent.

Mistress of the starry vault,
the vast cathedral of the sky;
forgive thy servant every fault,
before the day that I must die.

Let me remember only good;
the anguished ecstasy of grace.
Grant me, by thy lovely name,
the vision splendid of thy face.

Thy servant worshipped as of old
his fathers did, by ancient rites.
By power of love and magick bold,
keep sacred all thy holy nights.

Now vision dimmed, enfeebled flame
of life, at last the time has come
to leave this old and worn out frame,
so mote it be and be it done!

By Ishtar and by Ea, by the countless names of power,
reborn thy servant dances about the time-worn tower.
The altar fire is lit again, the incense fumes arise;
once more thy holy rites are run beneath the moonlit skies.

Let the candles burn for half an hour before extinguishing them. Repeat every night for seven nights.

It is possible to obtain very large, long-burning candles. These should, if possible, be used for the astral and light blue candles in this ritual.

DREAMS

ALTAR 1   FIGURE   ALTAR 2
CENSER

LIGHT BLUE   WHITE

PETITIONER

ORANGE

BOOK   DAY
CANDLE

To Cause Dreams

Light altar candles 1 and 2.

Light day candle.

Light incense.

Light petitioner's candle, saying:

Here is . . . (name) . . . , the subject of this rite.

Light light blue candle and say:

Here burn tranquility and patience,
necessary for the accomplishment of the desire.

Light orange candle and say:

Here is the attraction of that desire,
that she/he may dream the dreams
she/he would wish
and see and experience all that she/he wills.

Light white candle and say:

For truth in all that she/he sees, is this flame lit.

Close your eyes for a moment and see the petitioner
(or yourself) completely surrounded and enveloped in
a white light. After a few minutes of this, open your
eyes again and say:

Whence comes the wind that blows softly through the trees?
And whither doth it go?
Yet in its gentle passing do we not feel
its soft velvet touch upon our cheek?
Like the flutter of a butterfly's wings,
now sensed; now lost!
For all its reality we cannot reach out and touch,
and grasp, the wind.
It is there; yet it is not!
How real too is our sense of sight
when we see, in dreams, the ones we love.
Again we see them and talk with them,
and walk and love again.

Yet are they there?
Will they come when we call?
Can we see and do what we will?
Yes, and yes again. 'Tis true!
All that which we desire to see, to experience,
in our dreams, is ours for the asking.
Will, and it shall come!
Ask, and it shall be given!
Know that the power is within us,
and all that we desire shall be ours!

Sit quietly for a few moments before extinguishing the candles. This ritual should be performed at night, before going to bed, when dreams are desired.

ENEMY

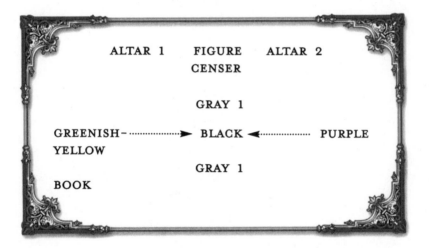

ALTAR 1   FIGURE   ALTAR 2
           CENSER

           GRAY 1

GREENISH-········▶ BLACK ◀········ PURPLE
YELLOW
           GRAY 1

BOOK

To Bring Pressure to Bear on an Enemy

Light altar candles 1 and 2.

Light incense.

Light black candle and say:

> *Here stands mine enemy, all alone.*
> *He/she is without friend,*
> *without help . . . (name). . . , I pity thee.*
> *Soon will you pay for tormenting me.*

Light gray 1 and 2, concentrating and saying:

Nought is before thee; nought is behind thee.
Frustration is at hand.
All thine plans are as nought.
Thou hast no plans.

Light greenish-yellow, concentrating and saying:

Here is the sickness, doubt, and worry
that is creeping in on you.
Fear, anger, and discord are your new companions.

Light purple candle, concentrate, and say:

Your other new-found friend is tension. Here be he.
To march also to thy side. Await his coming.

Sit for a moment getting, in your mind's eye, a clear picture of your enemy. Then say:

To the west, to the east,
to the north, to the south,
all around him/her the land
appears clear.
As he/she rides 'cross the plains
and cuts through the woods,
in an effort to just
disappear.
But behind all unseen
o'er the breast of a hill,
and beside him/her in bush

and in tree,
all the Little Folk track
him/her and keep a close watch
to ensure that he/she'll
ne'er get free.
They send signals by day,
they send signals by night,
they're alerted to where
he/she may go.
And all of the time
they will keep out of sight,
yet within reach of their
magick bows.
He/she comes out of a copse
and then pauses awhile
whilst the horse snorts her fear
of the men
she can sense are right there,
hidden safely away
from the sight of her rider.
But then
from the quiver and snort
of the horse he/she begins
to uneasily feel
what she knows;
that he/she's not, as once thought,
riding out of the land
where he/she slaughtered and made
many foes.

For now he/she must repay
what was stole from the Folk;
what he/she took without thought,
out of hand.
Now the fear that they had
has been turned back on him/her,
and he/she runs for his/her life
'cross the land.
He/she puts spurs to the steed
and catches the scent
of the terrors that now
become his/hers.
For the seekers now sought,
yes, the Hunter is chas'd,
and it's sure that revenge
will not miss.
He/she no longer looks back
as he/she crouches and rides
at full gallop, no longer
with care
what direction he/she takes
just so long as there's speed
that can take him/her away
from their stares.
But there is no escape
for a one of his/her kind
Though he/she run on for

shelter to find.
Rides there Fear at his/her side
and rides Death in his/her heart
and there's Panic so closely
behind.

Allow the candles to burn for five minutes before extinguishing them. Repeat the ritual on successive nights, each time moving the greenish-yellow and purple candles two inches closer toward the black.

EVIL

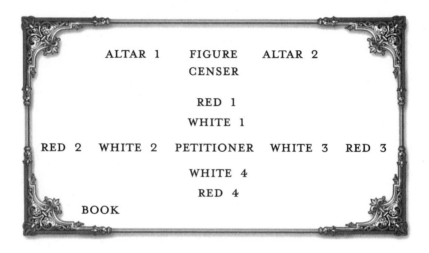

```
         ALTAR 1      FIGURE      ALTAR 2
                      CENSER

                      RED  1
                      WHITE  1

RED  2   WHITE  2   PETITIONER   WHITE  3   RED  3

                      WHITE  4
                      RED  4

         BOOK
```

To Protect against Evil

To "Uncross" a Person

Light altar candles 1 and 2.

Light incense, preferably frankincense.

Light petitioner's candle, thinking hard of the petitioner dressed all in white.

Light white candles 1, 2, 3, and 4, saying:

Here is a circle of purity about the spark of . . . (name) . . .
whose spirit burns brightly in the midst.
It is an ever-present protection for her/him;
It is the greatest purifier.

Light red candles 1, 2, 3 and 4, saying:

Reinforcing the circle of purity is a further circle of strength.
Spiritual strength for . . . (name) . . . .
She/he is protected from all harm; all evil.
She/he is purified and born again.

Think of the petitioner as happy and carefree,
with no evil about the petitioner and no fear of any
such evil. After a few minutes say:

There is a god of whom my prayers,
poor as I am, no boon request;
I watch the world and its affairs,
cherish the good, forget the rest;
and pleasure, howe'er priests may prate,
my modest creed does not offend,
gaily I drink, and leave my fate
to god, the good folk's friend!

Beside my pillow poverty
sits brooding, but I heed her not,
for thanks to love and hope, you see,
I dream a bed of down my lot.
Mine no stern god that priests create,

gentle is he to whom I bend;
gaily I drink, and leave my fate
to god, the good folk's friend!

A conquering despot drunk with power,
nations and dynasties down flings,
the dust his charger's proud hoofs shower
begrimes the sacred brows of kings.
Crawl on, crawl on, ye fallen great,
what reck I how your glories end?
Gaily I drink, and leave my fate
to god, the good folk's friend!

Oh, our foreboding friend the priest,
with all his prophesies of gloom!
On hell-fire how he loves to feast,
the end of time, the crack of doom!
Come, Ceridwen, your cheeks inflate,
in flame and thunder-cloud descend!
Gaily I drink, and leave my fate
to god, the good folk's friend!

What, god a god of anger? Pooh,
he made all and loves all he made;
the wine he gives; my dear friends, you;
love which is his creating aid;
the charms of all these dissipate
the nightmares priests rejoice to send!
Gaily I drink, and leave my fate
to my god, the good folk's friend.

Sit then and think of all evil evaporating. See the petitioner free and happy. Sit thinking thus until the candles have burned right down and finally go out.

FEAR

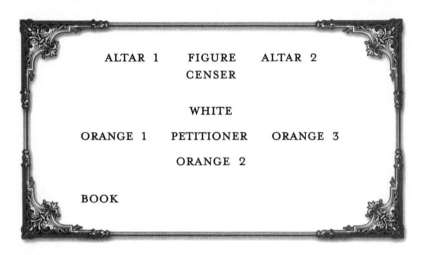

ALTAR 1	FIGURE	ALTAR 2
	CENSER	
	WHITE	
ORANGE 1	PETITIONER	ORANGE 3
	ORANGE 2	
BOOK		

To Conquer Fear

Light altar candles 1 and 2.

Light incense.

Sit and meditate on what is to be done.

Light the petitioner's candle, concentrating your thoughts on the petitioner and saying:

This candle represents . . . (name) . . .
whose spirit burns as surely and as steadfastly as this flame.

Light white candle and say:

Here is added confidence and strength for . . . (name) . . . ;
purity and sincerity are with him/her always.

Light the orange candles in order, saying:

Here is found the necessary will to overcome all fear.
As burn these candles so burns
the indomitable heart of . . . (name) . . .
that . . . (name) . . . may grasp his or her ideal
and be rid of doubts;
that . . . (name) . . . may conquer all.

Sit then in contemplation, thinking of the fear
dispelling and the confidence growing. After three
or four minutes stand and say:

I was afraid and alone; or so I felt.
Fear I knew.
I was without heart, for weak was I,
down in the darkness without knowledge.
Fear I knew.
The snap of teeth, the thunder of the herd,
the trample and the swirl,
the sounds, the sights
in thought . . .
fear I knew.
Yet the time came and is come,
for all about now fled.

Laugh is the word, and laugh the sword
to fill my heart and grasp upon.
No fear I know; no doubt, no woe;
not now.
With strength, and joy, with gladness in my heart
that fear I knew is far behind me now.
Forward the light; no dark about;
no fright, no fear in sight.
I am the one and all toward me look
and see—I have no fear!

Extinguish the candles.

Repeat every night for nine nights.

HAPPINESS

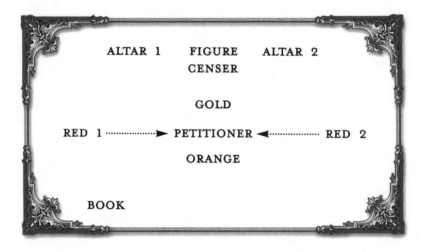

```
        ALTAR 1      FIGURE      ALTAR 2
                     CENSER

                      GOLD

RED  1 ·············▶ PETITIONER ◀············· RED  2

                     ORANGE


        BOOK
```

To Win or Hold Happiness

Light altar candles 1 and 2.

Light incense.

Light petitioner's candle, thinking of the petitioner, and say:

> *Here stands . . . (name) . . . ,*
> *her/his spirit as steadfast as this flame.*
> *Happiness is hers/his, well deserved.*

Light gold and orange candles and say:

Happiness is attracted to . . . (name) . . .
as a moth is attracted to such a flame as this.
The attraction is so great it cannot be resisted.
It draws; it pulls.

Light red candles 1 and 2 and say:

Here is the luck and happiness she/he deserves.
She/he has worked hard for it; it is rightly hers/his.
It swings toward her/him and advances.
It is hers/his to own.

Think now of the person obtaining all that she or he desires, and say:

A star dawns beauteous in my gloomy night,
a star that sheds sweet comfort with its light,
promising me new life and joy— oh, do not lie!

Like as the ocean to the moon swells free,
so mounts my soul, daring and glad to thee—
to thee, and to thy light of joy— oh, do not lie!

Think, for a few minutes, of the happiness building, then say again:

A star dawns beauteous in my gloomy night,
a star that sheds sweet comfort with its light,
promising me new life and joy— oh, do not lie!

Like as the ocean to the moon swells free,
so mounts my soul, daring and glad to thee—
to thee, and to thy light of joy— oh, do not lie!

Concentrate, for a few further minutes, on the happiness growing and building. Then say again:

> *A star dawns beauteous in my gloomy night,*
> *a star that sheds sweet comfort with its light,*
> *promising me new life and joy— oh, do not lie!*

> *Like as the ocean to the moon swells free,*
> *so mounts my soul, daring and glad to thee—*
> *to thee, and to thy light of joy— oh, do not lie!*

Sit for a further few minutes before extinguishing the candles.

Repeat the ritual successive nights, each time moving the red candles two inches in toward the petitioner. Continue until the three touch one another.

HEALING

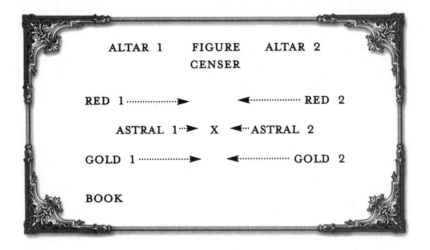

ALTAR 1   FIGURE   ALTAR 2
CENSER

RED 1 ·················▶   ◀················· RED 2

ASTRAL 1···▶ X ◀···ASTRAL 2

GOLD 1 ·················▶   ◀················· GOLD 2

BOOK

To Heal an Unhappy Marriage

Light altar candles 1 and 2.

Light incense.

Meditate on what is to be done.

Light astral 1, red 1, gold 1, while thinking of the husband. Say:

> *The husband of this marriage is . . . (name) . . .*
>
> *whose spirit I light*

symbolically in the knowledge that
he will strengthen and
grow in his love for his wife, . . . (name). . . .

Light astral 2, red 2, gold 2, while thinking of
the wife. Say:

The wife of this marriage is . . . (name) . . .
whose spirit I light symbolically
in the knowledge that she will strengthen and
grow in her love for her husband, . . . (name). . . .

Sit then for five minutes thinking of the two
being drawn together. Then say:

Together, together, together;
healed are the rifts between them.
Warm is the light that springs across
the gulf that is no more.

Happiness steals upon the scene,
for love is the word and love is the light.
Differences forgotten; unthinking words erased.
Love is the salve that heals all hurts.

A further five minutes of contemplation; then
repeat:

Together, together, together;
healed are the rifts between them.
Warm is the light that springs across
the gulf that is no more.

Happiness steals upon the scene,
for love is the word and love is the light.
Differences forgotten; unthinking words erased.
Love is the salve that heals all hurts.

A final five minutes of contemplation; then again:

Together, together, together;
healed are the rifts between them.
Warm is the light that springs across
the gulf that is no more.

Happiness steals upon the scene,
for love is the word and love is the light.
Differences forgotten; unthinking words erased.
Love is the salve that heals all hurts.

Allow candles to burn a further five minutes, then extinguish them.

Repeat every other day, first moving the two sets of candles one inch toward each other. Continue until two astral candles touch.

HEALTH

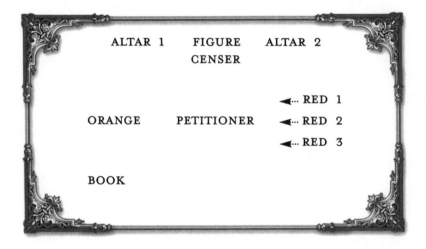

ALTAR 1   FIGURE   ALTAR 2
CENSER

◄··· RED 1

ORANGE   PETITIONER   ◄··· RED 2

◄··· RED 3

BOOK

To Regain (or Retain) Good Health

Light altar candles 1 and 2. Light incense.

If this ritual is done to regain health, sit for a few moments thinking of the goodness and health flowing back into the body.

Light petitioner's candle, picturing petitioner. Say:

Here is . . . (name) . . . , in excellent health.
The blessings of the gods be upon him/her
that he/she may prosper.

Light orange candle and say:

This flame draws all that is good to . . . (name). . . .
It draws health and strength and all that he/she desires.

Light red 1, 2, and 3 and say:

Here, then, is that health and strength, threefold.
It is here to be taken into . . . (name) . . . 's body,
to serve him/her and build him/her as the gods would wish.

Then say:

And in the beginning was it ever thus.
That to live one must hunt; to kill.
That to kill must there be strength.
That for strength must there be eating and movement.
To eat and move must there be hunting.
Be you weak and you will never be strong.
Be you strong and so you shall remain.
But if you be weak, then must you think strong;
for thought is the deed.
And thinking strong can you then hunt and kill and eat.
Thus thinking strong you are strong and you move.
Thought brings not the food,
but thought doth bring the means to acquire the food.

So be it.
Strength to the strong.
Strength to the weak.
May the arm lift the spear.
May the arm hurl the stone.
May the arm thrust the javelin.
May there be strength, always.
So mote it be.

Sit quietly meditating on the wonderful good health enjoyed, and to be enjoyed, by the petitioner. Sit thus for ten to fifteen minutes, then extinguish the candles. Repeat this ritual every Friday evening for seven Fridays, each time moving the three red candles a little closer in toward the petitioner. On the seventh Friday they should touch.

JEALOUSY

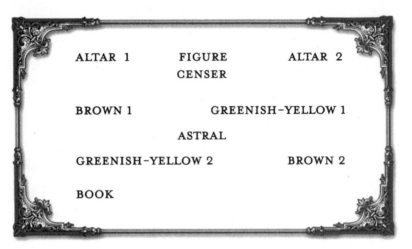

| ALTAR 1 | FIGURE | ALTAR 2 |
| CENSER | | |

| BROWN 1 | | GREENISH-YELLOW 1 |

ASTRAL

| GREENISH-YELLOW 2 | | BROWN 2 |

BOOK

To Arouse Jealousy

Light altar candles 1 and 2.

Light incense.

Light astral candle of the person in whom it is desired to arouse jealousy. Think intensely of her or him, and say:

Here is the woman/man . . . (name) . . . ; as this flame burns
so burns she/he, consumed with jealousy.

Light brown candles 1 and 2 and say:

> . . . *(name)* . . . *is uncertain.*
> *She/he is uncertain of herself/himself; of others.*
> *She/he hesitates—and will be lost.*

Light greenish-yellow candles 1 and 2 and say:

> *Jealousy is about her/him. It eats into her/him.*
> *It burns with a steady flame.*

Then, thinking of her or him growing more and
more jealous, say:

> *I lay and slept—a blessed sleep—*
> *it lulled my grief and care;*
> *when lo! A vision to me came,*
> *a maid divinely fair.*
>
> *As marble was the maiden pale,*
> *and wondrous to behold;*
> *her eyes were bright with pearly tears,*
> *her locks were waving gold.*
>
> *And lowly, lowly, gliding on,*
> *the maid as marble pale,*
> *she lies upon my heaving heart,*
> *the maid as marble pale.*
>
> *How thrills and throbs, with joy and pain,*
> *my heart in furious glow!*
> *Nor thrills nor throbs the maiden's breast—*
> *'tis cold as driven snow.*

"My bosom neither thrills nor throbs,
'tis ice-cold to the sense;
yet well I know the joys of love,
and love's omnipotence.

No rosy tinge is on my cheek,
and in my heart no blood;
yet struggle not with shuddering fear;
to thee I'm kind and good."

And wilder still she clings to me,
my senses 'gin to fail;
loud crows the cock—then melts in air
the maid as marble pale.

After a moment extinguish the candles. Perform the ritual every Monday and Saturday for three weeks.

LOVE

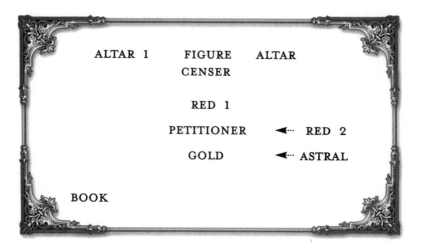

ALTAR 1   FIGURE   ALTAR
             CENSER

RED 1

PETITIONER   ◄⋯ RED 2

GOLD   ◄⋯ ASTRAL

BOOK

To Win the Love
of a Man or a Woman

Light altar candles 1 and 2.

Light incense.

Light candle of petitioner, saying:

> *Here is . . . (name). . . ,*
> *this candle is him/her;*
> *this flame burns as does his/her spirit.*

Light red 1 and say:

> *The love of . . . (name) . . . is great and is here shown.*
> *It is a good strong love and sought by many.*

Light astral candle of person whose love is desired, saying:

> *This is the heart of . . . (name) . . . whom here I see.*
> *I picture her/him before me and know her/him so.*

Light red 2 and say:

> *The love . . . (name) . . . has for*
> *. . . (petitioner's name) . . . grows with this flame.*
> *It burns as does the light*
> *and is forever drawn toward him/her.*
> *Great is the love he/she has for her/him.*

Light gold candle and say:

> *Here draws she to he; the one toward the other.*
> *Such is his/her love that all feel its attraction.*
> *This candle burns and draws her/him ever near.*
> *Powerful is his/her persuasion.*
> *Ever does she/he feel the pull;*
> *the thought of him/her is constant.*
> *Her/his days are long with yearning for him/her,*
> *her/his nights are filled with desire.*
> *To be as one, together, is all that she/he would wish.*
> *To be as one, forever, is her/his immediate need.*
> *For no rest shall she/he find until*

beside him/her, she/he does lie.
His/her every wish she'll/he'll move to fill
to serve, to live—not die.
She/he cannot fight a pull so strong,
Nor would she/he think to fight;
she/he wishes but to ride the stream
to him/her, at journey's end.
Where the sun goes up
shall his/her love be by him/her;
where the sun goes down
there will she/he be.

Sit for a moment before extinguishing the candles.

Repeat the ritual every day, moving the astral and red 2 candles one inch toward the petitioner each time. Continue daily until astral and red 2 touch petitioner.

LUCK

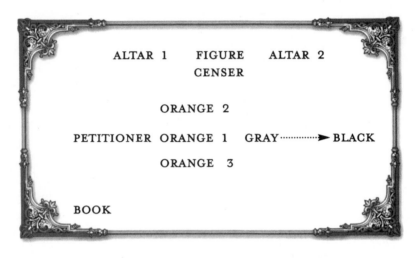

ALTAR 1   FIGURE   ALTAR 2
CENSER

ORANGE 2

PETITIONER ORANGE 1   GRAY ············► BLACK

ORANGE 3

BOOK

To Change One's Luck

Light altar candles 1 and 2.

Light incense.

Light petitioner's candle, thinking hard about petitioner and saying:

> *This candle represents . . . (name). . . .*
> *It represents her/him and is her/him in all things.*

Light orange 1, 2, and 3, thinking of the petitioner's luck changing for the better. Say:

Encouragement be to . . . (name) . . .
that her/his luck may change
and good fortune may be hers/his.

Light black candle and say:

Here is the bad luck that has been . . . (name) . . . 's.
All that went ill with her/him is here.
All the hardships and disappointments are herein.

Light gray candle thinking of the ill being cancelled out, and say:

Neutralize here the bad and the ill.
Let it come to a halt; then to swing about
and grow to the good.

Think of petitioner's luck definitely changing;
swinging from bad to good. Then think of it growing
on the good side. After a few moments thought, say:

What would you?
Why, to improve.
How improve?
To gain, to live, to love.
Love you not now?
Yea and nay; for though I love I feel 'tis a morsel of a whole
which lies awaiting.
And so 'tis! What would you gain?
That very whole whereof I speak.
I face a wall;
I am in an alley blind. Lead me from hence.
To life? To love?

Yea; to that, and more.
More, *you say? You have ambition!*
Indeed I have, for my luck must I change
that I may proceed.
That you have that ambition is the key.
Success shall be yours. But when?
Patience! That you must have.
I have it; is't enough?
With ambition, yes, if ye truly have the two.
For they go not well together.
When, then, might I find this change?
When will my luck improve?
Within the moon, that I vow.
Retain within you the thought that all will be well.
You will improve.
You have much to live; and much to love.
Relax not your ambition, neither discouraged be.
Through the changing phases of Our Lady*
will you see these plans fulfilled until, at last,
you will give no thought to the past.
How so?
You will be too busy with the future.

Sit for ten minutes thinking of all things changing for the better.

Extinguish the candles.

Repeat the ritual on successive nights, each time moving the gray candle one inch closer to the black.

* The moon.

MEDITATION

```
        ALTAR 1      FIGURE     ALTAR 2
                     CENSER


LIGHT BLUE 1      PETITIONER/      LIGHT BLUE 2
                   MEDITATOR


     BOOK                      DAY CANDLE
```

To Meditate

Light altar candles 1 and 2.

Light incense.

Light day candle.

Light petitioner's candle (petitioner = meditator),
thinking of yourself, and say:

This candle is myself, burning steady and true.

Light light blue candles 1 and 2, and say:

Here do I find peace and tranquility.
A place apart where I may safely meditate
and grow in spirituality.

Settle into meditation in your own particular pattern (i.e., transcendental meditation, mantric yoga, or whatever).* At end of meditation period extinguish candles, reversing the order of lighting.

---

* Some recommended books on meditation: *The TM Book* by Denise Denniston and Peter McWilliams; *Meditate the Tantric Yoga Way* by Swami Jyotirmayananda; *Buddhist Meditation* by G. Constant Lounsberry; and *Why and How of Meditation* by Russ Michael.

MONEY

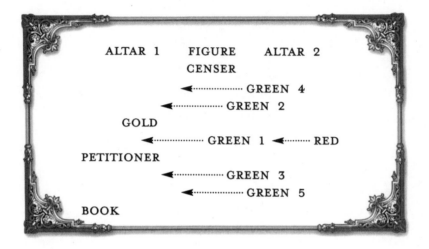

```
    ALTAR 1      FIGURE      ALTAR 2
                 CENSER
                 ◄············· GREEN  4
              ◄············· GREEN  2
       GOLD
              ◄············· GREEN  1  ◄········· RED
   PETITIONER
              ◄············· GREEN  3
              ◄············· GREEN  5
    BOOK
```

To Obtain Money

Light altar candies I and 2.

Light incense.

Sit for a moment and meditate. Get clear in your mind just what you wish to accomplish.

Light petitioner's candle, thinking hard on the petitioner (it may well be yourself, of course). You then say:

This candle represents . . . (petitioner's name). . . .
As it burns, so burns his/her spirit.

Light gold candle. Think hard on attraction, and say:

This candle represents attraction.
It works with and for . . . (petitioner's name) . . .
the name beside it.

Light the green candles in order, thinking hard on money. As you light them say:

These candles represent the money that
. . . (petitioner's name) . . . desires.
It is as much as he/she needs* —no more, and no less.

Light the red candle, thinking of the complete wish fulfilled.

This candle represents the power and the command
to drive the money to . . . (petitioner's name). . . .

Pause, then, a moment to reflect. Then say:

As money is necessary to the fulfillment of our needs,
so must we ever strive to obtain it.
All should be earned or not received at all.
The need of . . . (name) . . . at present is intense.
Draw, then, money to him/her.
Let him/her find all that he/she shall need.
Supply, now, to meet his/her urgent want.

---

* You will find that this ritual will bring money when it is badly needed. It will not bring money just for the sake of having money.

For it is said the gods will provide
when surely is there a need.
Now is that need. Let all work well for him/her.
Let him/her have sufficient.
Let him/her no longer have want.

Think now of the wish fulfilled, and the petitioner now having the money. Think of it actually being in his/her possession.

This money now is his/hers.
. . . (name) . . . holds it and has it,
and now it fills his/her need.
He/she has received it safely and is glad.
Praise be the gods for their goodness.
Ever is it thus.
Now all is well.

Sit then quietly for five minutes and let the candles and incense burn. At the end of this period, you may extinguish the flames.

The ritual should be repeated the following day, but before starting, move the five green candles and the red one two inches to the left of their previous positions. So move them each day before the ritual until they finally meet the stationary gold and petitioner's candles, with green I actually touching them.

NERVES

ALTAR 1   FIGURE   ALTAR 2
CENSER

ORANGE

PETITIONER

LIGHT BLUE 1   LIGHT BLUE 2

BOOK

To Soothe and Quiet the Nerves

Light the altar candles 1 and 2.

Light the incense.

Sit for a moment and try to clear the mind of all thoughts.

Light the petitioner's candle, and say:

> *Here, at peace, stands . . . (name) . . . ,*
> *her/his spirit as steadfast as the candle flame.*

Light the orange candle and say:

> *Here is encouragement in her/his endeavors.*
> *Here is strength to thrust aside her/his cares.*

Light the light blue candles 1 and 2 and say:

> *Around . . . (name) . . .*
> *are peace, tranquility, patience, and love.*

Sit for a moment in silence, then say, softly:

> *Soft is the rain, it gently falls*
> *upon the fields beneath.*
> *It lulls the heart, it stills the mind,*
> *gives solitude we seek.*
> *It patters down, so gentle yet*
> *it ne'er does bend a leaf,*
> *And yet the water that is there*
> *will wash away all grief.*
> *For smoothness follows in the wake,*
> *and quiet and peace and love*
> *are all around in freshness new,*
> *come down from clouds above.*
> *We feel so calm, so warm, so still;*
> *'tis never more that we*
> *will feel upset or "nerve-on-edge,"*
> *but keep tranquility.*
> *For love we now find all around,*
> *so soft, so still, so sure;*
> *we can relax, we can lie back,*
> *with peace and quiet as cure.*

Sit quietly for ten or fifteen minutes thinking of meadows and streams, woods, fields, and flowers. Keep your mind on pleasant things—objects rather than events. Then, once again, say:

> *Soft is the rain, it gently falls*
> *upon the fields beneath.*
> *It lulls the heart, it stills the mind,*
> *gives solitude we seek.*
> *It patters down, so gentle yet*
> *it ne'er does bend a leaf,*
> *and yet the water that is there*
> *will wash away all grief.*
> *For smoothness follows in the wake,*
> *and quiet and peace and love*
> *are all around in freshness new,*
> *come down from clouds above.*
> *We feel so calm, so warm, so still;*
> *'tis never more that we*
> *will feel upset or "nerve-on-edge,"*
> *but keep tranquility.*
> *For love we now find all around,*
> *so soft, so still, so sure;*
> *we can relax, we can lie back,*
> *with peace and quiet as cure.*

Extinguish the candles.

Repeat the ritual whenever you feel the need.

POWER

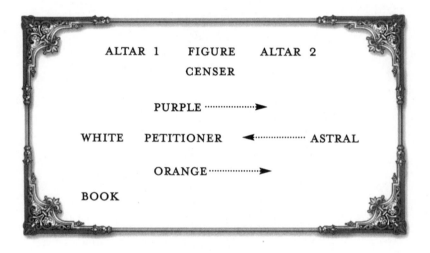

ALTAR 1   FIGURE   ALTAR 2
CENSER

PURPLE ················►

WHITE   PETITIONER ◄················ ASTRAL

ORANGE ················►

BOOK

To Gain Power over Others

Light altar candles 1 and 2.

Light incense, and as the smoke rises, think of petitioner's power rising with it.

Light petitioner's candle, thinking of petitioner, and say:

> *Here burns the spirit, the might and power,*
> *of . . . (name). . . .*

He/she has a strength to overcome all.

Light the white candle and say:

Here is the strength of . . . (name). . . .
Here is the purity and sincerity that will make
. . . (name) . . .
master of all who oppose him/her.

Light astral candle of the one whom petitioner wishes to dominate. Say:

I see before me the figure of . . . (name) . . . ,
servant to . . . (petitioner's name). . . .
Nothing can he/she do without
his/her master's wish.
Nothing can he/she think
without his master's instruction.
For he/she is but a puppet in his/her master's hands.

Light the purple candle and say:

Power be to . . . (name). . . .

Light orange candle and say:

Attraction is his/hers;
he/she draws others to him/her
and to his/her will.

Sit for a few moments and think of the other person actually running hither and thither at the whim of the petitioner. Say:

For he/she is a god/goddess; there is none his/her equal,
and there is none other who surpasses him/her.
He/she is a master of understanding,
excellent in plans and beneficent of decrees;
and going and coming are according to his/her commands.
He/she it was who subdued the foreign lands
while his/her father was within the palace;
and he/she reported to him that what
he/she was ordered had been done.
Mighty indeed is he/she, achieving with his/her strong arm;
a valiant one, and there is not his/her equal!
He/she slakes his/her wrath by smashing skulls;
and no one can stand up about him/her.
He/she is robust of heart at the moment of attack;
and does not let sloth rest upon his/her heart.
Bold of countenance is he/she when seeing the melee;
to attack the barbarian is his/her joy.
He/she girds his shield and crushes the foe;
and does not strike twice in order to kill!
But he/she is lord of charm and great of sweetness;
and through love has he/she conquered!
His/her city loves him/her more than itself;
it rejoices in him/her more than in its god;
men and women salute and rejoice with him/her
now that he/she is king/queen!
He/she conquered while still in the egg.
And his/her face was turned to royal deeds
since he/she was born.

He/she makes multiply those who were born with him/her;
he/she is unique, the gift of the god.
He/she is one who makes wide the boundaries;
he/she will seize the southern countries,
and the northern ones with ease,
having been created to smite the Syrians
and to crush the sand-crossers.
How this land rejoices now that he/she is come to rule!

Extinguish the candles.

Repeat every night for nine nights. Each time move the astral candle one inch in toward the center; also move the purple and orange candles one inch in toward the center.

—❦ POWER INCREASE ❦—

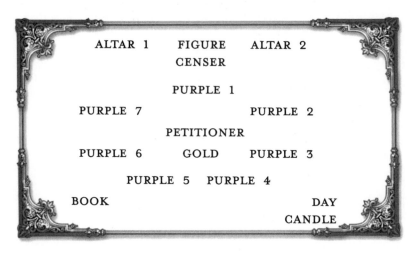

ALTAR 1	FIGURE	ALTAR 2
	CENSER	
	PURPLE 1	
PURPLE 7		PURPLE 2
	PETITIONER	
PURPLE 6	GOLD	PURPLE 3
	PURPLE 5 PURPLE 4	
BOOK		DAY
		CANDLE

To Increase Your Power*

Light altar candles I and 2. Light incense.

Light petitioner's candle, thinking hard about petitioner, and say:

> Here stands . . . (name) . . . , a person of power.
> She/he possesses great potential,
> which but awaits the signal to appear.

---

* Good for scrying powers, magickal powers, healing powers, ESP, etc.

Light gold (or yellow) candle, and say:

> *This is the flame of attraction, and of confidence.*
> *Through it will her/his potential be realized.*

Light the day candle. (*Note:* This ritual should be started seven days before the full moon. The day candle is of the appropriate color for the ritual day (see table 2, page 11) and will therefore, of course, be a different candle each day the ritual is performed.)

Light purple candle 1. (*Note:* On the second day of the ritual light purple candles 1 and 2; the third day, purple candles 1, 2, and 3; and so on.) Say:

> *The power within . . . (name) . . .*
> *burns steady as a flame,*
> *increasing in strength as day follows day.*
> *Ever is it present; ever may it be used.*
> *For however much is drawn off*
> *so is it replenished threefold.*

Sit, or kneel comfortably, and meditate on petitioner, seeing the petitioner's power—be it healing, ESP, magickal, or whatever—growing and growing. In your mind picture petitioner surrounded by a deep purple light or mist. See this light building in size and density, then see it being absorbed into petitioner. No sooner is it absorbed than more develops, to be absorbed in turn. Keep up this concentrated meditation for as long as you are able, then relax and clear your mind completely. Say:

So grows the power for . . . (name) . . . ,
ever increasing and ever replenished.
As day follows day, so does the power grow.
The more it is used, the more it grows in strength.
Let it be ever thus.

Extinguish the candles, reversing the order of lighting.

PROSPERITY

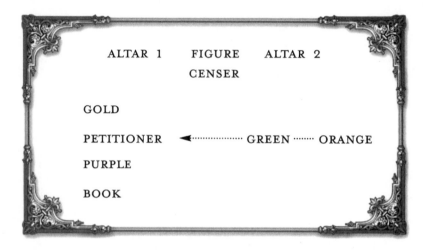

ALTAR 1	FIGURE	ALTAR 2
	CENSER	
GOLD		
PETITIONER ◄········· GREEN ······· ORANGE		
PURPLE		
BOOK		

To Gain Prosperity

Light altar candles 1 and 2. Light incense.

Think, for a few moments, of the petitioner growing more and more prosperous; through the petitioner's own efforts, of course.

Light the petitioner's candle and think hard on her or him. Say:

> *This candle represents . . . (name) . . .*
> *whose spirit and determination*
> *are as strong and true as this flame.*

Light gold candle and say:

> Here is the confidence of . . . (name). . . .
> It is such that it cannot help but
> draw prosperity to him/her.

Light purple candle and say:

> This is the flame of power.
> It must be handled carefully.
> But if so handled it will reward its handler with wealth and
> prosperity beyond his/her dreams.
> It is progress—upward.

Light both the green and the orange candles (green first), and say:

> Here are to be found the monies of the world.
> Here is true prosperity; true wealth and good fortune.

Then say:

> The little spring upon the hill splashes forth the crystal flow.
> Down from the height it rushes,
> gathering to it as it runs the many
> lesser streams that seek release.
> It grows and grows; a rushing, ever-widening stream.
> On the plains it slows but still does it grow.
> Sucking in all it touches;
> absorbing lesser flows to feed itself.
> Gaining, gaining, ever spreading. Growing.
> At last, at long long last, the sea is reached.

That vast expanse that stretches out and reaches
past the horizon to eternity.
Pausing not at all the rushing river wades right in—
absorbed? . . . Or all absorbing? Possessed? . . .
Or finally possessing all?
Thus did it grow, from humblest beginnings
until it owned the all. The whole.
The one.

Sit for a while before extinguishing the candles. Repeat the ritual successive days, moving the green and orange candles two inches toward the petitioner each time.

Continue until the green and the petitioner's candles touch.

PURIFICATION

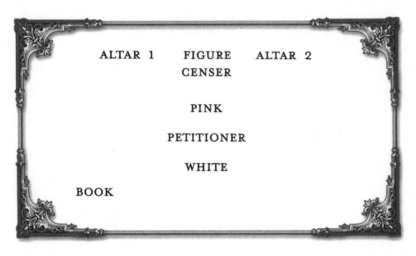

ALTAR 1   FIGURE   ALTAR 2
CENSER

PINK

PETITIONER

WHITE

BOOK

To Purify Oneself

Light altar candles 1 and 2.

Light incense.

Light petitioner's candle whilst concentrating your thoughts on petitioner, and say:

Here stands . . . (name) . . . ,
whose spirit burns as truly as does this flame.
She/he is upstanding, steadfast, and true.
Purity is her/his name.

Light pink candle whilst thinking of petitioner's great love and honor. Say:

Here is her/his honor, her/his righteousness.

Light white candle and say:

And here also is her/his purity, sincerity.

Now think hard of all these qualities entering into the petitioner *and remaining there.* They are now a part of the petitioner. The petitioner is purity. Say:

The high priestess, attended by her handmaidens,
came from out of the east and arrived
at last at the banks of the stream.
There did she pause and,
her eyes reflecting the glimmering
of the waters,
she smiled and lifted her arms to the skies.
Her handmaidens approached her;
with musical laughter
they began to remove their lady's garments.
The delicate silken scarfs they laid
upon the dewed grass beside the stream,
and on them placed the high priestess' **bigghes***.
As the youngest of them brushed out her mistress' hair
the others removed their own garments.
Then did they all clasp hands and,

---

* Ritual jewels.

with little cries and gasps of delight,
run down the bank and into the silvery stream.

There did they splash and run and jump and cry;
water nymphs, sprites all.
The dusts of their journeys fell from their bodies.
Fell with them the dross of their cares.
Cleansed were they as they played in that sparkling
ribbon of water, wending twixt its grass- and tree-clad banks.
Cleansed were they, and pure again.

Sit quietly contemplating for fifteen minutes before extinguishing the candles.

Repeat the ritual every three days for as long as desired.

SCRYING

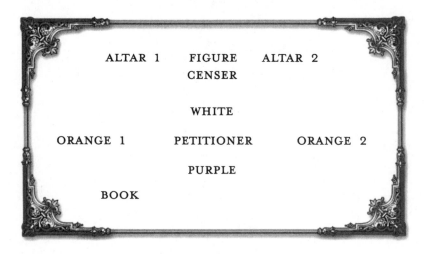

ALTAR 1   FIGURE   ALTAR 2
CENSER

WHITE

ORANGE 1   PETITIONER   ORANGE 2

PURPLE

BOOK

For Scrying*

Light altar candles 1 and 2.

Light incense (a mixture of cinnamon and mastic is recommended).

Light petitioner's candle, thinking of the petitioner, and say:

Here burns the spirit and the power of . . . (name) . . . ,
wise in the occult and steadfast in purity.

---

* Equally suitable for crystal gazing, mirror gazing, or any other form of the scrying art.

Light the white candle and say:

> *Here burn purity, truth, and sincerity.*
> *They are with him/her throughout this rite and beyond it.*

Light the purple candle and say:

> *Power is his/hers.*
> *Power to accomplish his/her ends in this rite.*

Light orange candles 1 and 2 and say:

> *That which he/she would scry is attracted to him/her*
> *as is the moth drawn to the candle flame.*

Sit for a moment and organize your thoughts. Decide exactly what it is you wish to see, then say:

> *Around me is built a wall of light;*
> *through it may pass only that which will harm me not.*
> *That I may see all there is no question,*
> *Yet aught I see may not reach out to me.*
> *The gods are my guides as they are my strength.*
> *All that is revealed is brought through them;*
> *for this do I give thanks.*

Turn your back to the illuminated altar and, clearing your mind of all thoughts, bring your attention to the object of your scrying (crystal, mirror, or whatever), which may be either on the floor or on another small table.

After scrying, turn once more to the altar and say:

That which was desired has been accomplished.
May the gods ever be with me
and protect me in aught I do.

Extinguish the candles, reversing the order of lighting.

SLANDER

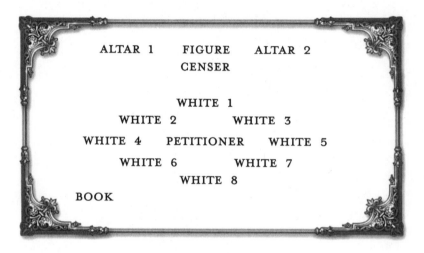

ALTAR 1   FIGURE   ALTAR 2

CENSER

WHITE 1

WHITE 2   WHITE 3

WHITE 4   PETITIONER   WHITE 5

WHITE 6   WHITE 7

WHITE 8

BOOK

To Stop Slander

Light altar candles 1 and 2.

Light incense.

Light petitioner's candle and concentrate your thoughts on her or him. Say:

Here stands . . . (name) . . . , unjustly slandered.

Light the white candles in order and say:

About her/him is truth and purity.
All around her/him is the power of honesty.
Nothing shall pass through this shield to harm her/him.

Imagine then that the unjust slander has stopped and that the petitioner has emerged clean and unscathed. Say loudly and boldly:

Here is an image I have made!
It is . . . (person's name) . . .
who spreads slander against me.
See, then, that it is she/he.
Now I have her/him here before me;
she/he who would do me evil.
Yet will I bind her/him and cast her/him down!
From the mouth where she/he speaks
that surely will I close;
will I sew together the lips
that they may speak no more.
Her/his body will I bind about
with redden cords so tight.
Close shall she/he be held
that nevermore may she/he speak;
nor in any way communicate her/his evil mind
to those who devour such things;
who masticate and pass them ever on
to sow the seeds of slander,
nurture, and wildly harvest.
Cut down, now, are their crops.

Barren are their fields.
Sterile is their land.
Stayed are the tongues;
close are the lips;
silenced are the thoughts
that my actions may go unscathed.
Be it ever thus,
for so is my will.

Sit in quiet contemplation for ten minutes before extinguishing the candles.

Repeat every three nights for as long as desired.

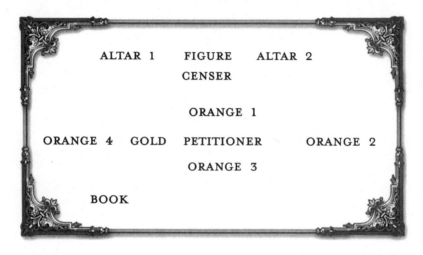

ALTAR 1   FIGURE   ALTAR 2
CENSER

ORANGE 1

ORANGE 4   GOLD   PETITIONER   ORANGE 2

ORANGE 3

BOOK

To Attain Success

Light altar candles 1 and 2.

Light incense and meditate on what success has to be attained.

Light petitioner's candle, picturing the petitioner, and say:

> *Here stands . . . (name) . . . ,*
> *a good and upright person.*
> *He/she works hard to attain success in*

. . . (detail that in which he/she wishes to attain success). . . .
Such success is richly deserved.

Light gold candle and say:

Here is the flame that will draw success to him/her.
Powerful is the flame; strong is the attraction.

Light orange candle 1 and say:

Here is the success he/she desires.
It is drawn to him/her by his/her own strength
and that of the gods.
It will come to him/her as strongly as he/she deserves it.
The more he/she works for success, the richer will it be.

Sit for five minutes thinking of all that the petitioner has done to deserve success in his or her undertaking. See the petitioner working for it. See it coming to the petitioner. See, now, the success all about the petitioner. See the petitioner finally being able to sit back and reap his or her just rewards. Say:

The sunbeams were playing
lightly over the billowy ocean;
far out at sea I saw shining the ship
that was to bear me homeward;
but the right wind as yet was wanting,
and tranquilly on the white sands I was sitting
by the lonely sea,
and I read the song of Ulysses,
that old, that ever youthful song,

from whose ocean-murmuring leaves
rose joyfully the breath of the gods,
and the sunny spring of humankind,
and the cloudless sky of fair Hellas.

My noble and faithful heart accompanied
the son of Laertes in toil and disaster:
it sat down with him, grieving in spirit,
at kindly hearths,
where queens sat spinning deep rich purple;
it helped him to lie and to escape deftly
from giants' caves and from nymphs' white arms;
it followed him into Kimmerian night.
Through storm and through shipwreck,
and suffered with him unspeakable anguish.

Sighing said I, "Revengeful Poseidon,
thy anger is awful, and myself am afraid
of my own return home."

Scarcely had I spoken the words,
when the sea foamed up high,
and from the white-crested billows arose
the head of the god,
crowned with seaweed,
and cried he, contemptuous:
"Fear not, my dear little poet!

I've no intention to harm in the least
thy poor little bark,

nor frighten thee out of thy poor little wits
with too boist'rous rocking:
for thou, little poet, hast ever incensed me,

thou never hast shaken the smallest turret
of the holy city of Priam;
nor hast thou singed e'en a single hair
from the eye of my son Polyphemus;
and never as yet has the goddess of wisdom,
Pallas Athenae, stood counselling beside thee."

Thus cried out Poseidon,
and dived back into the ocean;
and at the vulgar old sailor's joke
I heard Amphitrite, the coarse fish-woman,
and the silly daughters of Nereus,
giggling beneath the waters.

Sit for ten minutes picturing complete success for the petitioner.

Then extinguish the candles.

This ritual should first be done on a Tuesday. Repeat on Friday but then light orange candles 1 and 2. The following Tuesday do the ritual again lighting orange candles 1, 2, and 3. Finally, on the second Friday, do the ritual once more, lighting all four of the orange candles. The ritual may then be repeated every Tuesday and Friday, always lighting all candles, until complete success is attained.

TRUTH

ALTAR 1   FIGURE   ALTAR 2
CENSER

WHITE 1

PETITIONER

WHITE 2   WHITE 3

BOOK

To Learn the Truth

Light altar candles 1 and 2.

Light incense.

Think hard on the subject about which you wish to learn the truth.

Light petitioner's candle, thinking of petitioner and saying:

This candle I light to represent . . . (name). . . .
It burns as does her/his spirit. It is as her/him in all things.

94

Light the white candles in order, saying:

> *These are the symbols of truth.*
> *They are enjoined about . . . (name) . . .*
> *And to her/him show all truth.*

Then say:

> *As I rode in the night 'cross the brown heath bare,*
> *in the bright moon's light saw a castle fair;*
> *lords and ladies, great and small,*
> *were crowding in, 'twas a festival;*
> *grasses in the wind are waving.*
>
> *They bade me welcome and in I went*
> *to drink their wine to my heart's content.*
> *I danced and laughed with ladies fair.*
> *Ne'er in my life had I such cheer;*
> *grasses in the wind are waving.*
>
> *Then all at once there came a cry:*
> Haro by yaro! *Asleep fell I,*
> *while a lady dancing at my side*
> *seemed like a lizard away to glide;*
> *grasses in the wind are waving.*
>
> *I woke in the early light of day,*
> *in an olden ruin I did lay,*
> *o'er the rock and into the sun*
> *I saw a green-gold lizard run!*
> *Grasses in the wind are waving.*

Now the truth I know and it stays with me,
for I have seen what I did see,
all secret knowledge came to mind,
borne on the laughter of the other kind;
grasses in the wind are waving.

Sit then in quiet contemplation for half an hour. In this time will the truth of the subject in question come to you.

Extinguish the candles.

UNCROSSING

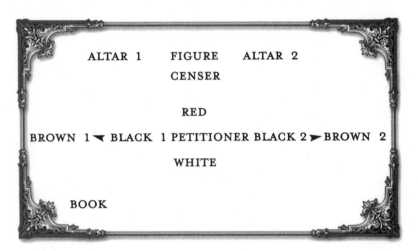

ALTAR 1   FIGURE   ALTAR 2

CENSER

RED

BROWN 1 ◄ BLACK 1 PETITIONER BLACK 2 ► BROWN 2

WHITE

BOOK

To Uncross a Person

Light altar candles 1 and 2.

Light incense.

Light petitioner's candle whilst thinking of petitioner. Say:

> *Here stands . . . (name) . . .*
> *who suffers under a crossed condition.*
> *Despite it his/her spirit burns as truly as doth this flame.*
> *Soon shall it be free.*

Light red candle and say:

> *Here, then, is strength, to endure all that may come;*
> *to recover all that has slipped by the way.*

Light white candle and say:

> *And here find we purity;*
> *the purity of . . . (name) . . .*
> *that shall emerge again, to reign forever.*

Light black candles 1 and 2 and say:

> *The blackness that surrounds . . . (petitioner's name) . . .*
> *is all enclosed about with these two candles.*
> *As the flames burn so is that blackness absorbed into them.*
> *As they are moved away from him/her,*
> *so is that blackness dispersed.*

Alternatively, if you know the name of the person* who has crossed the petitioner, say:

> *In these two candles find we the heart*
> *and the will of . . . (other name) . . . who crosses us.*
> *As the flames burn so is the blackness within him/her*
> *absorbed by them.*
> *As the candles are moved away,*
> *so moves the blackness with them.*

Light the brown candles 1 and 2 and say:

> *Here is uncertainty.*
> *No longer is there confidence in the evil mind.*

---

* Astral candles may be used rather than black ones, if the person is known.

No longer is the aim sure and steadfast.
Enters here doubt—and despair.

Think of the petitioner now being completely freed from his or her crossed position. Think hard on this and say:

Flow forth, poison,
thou of black and devious means!
Come hither at my utterance, according as I say!
I am the god who came into being of himself!
Come, issue forth at the command of Ceridwen;
I am Leif, the physician soothing the god.
Flow forth from the limbs!
Come, issue forth at the command of Arranrod;
Behold, I am Leif, the physician soothing the god.
Flow forth from the limbs!
Come, issue forth at the command of Bride;
Behold, I am Leif, the physician soothing the god.
Flow forth from the limbs!
Come, issue forth at the command of Astarte;
Behold, I am Leif, the physician soothing the god.
Flow forth from the limbs!
Come, issue forth at the command of Gana;
Behold, I am Leif, the physician soothing the god.
Flow forth from the limbs!

As the sun shall rise and cross the roof of the world;
as the services shall be performed
in every temple in the land;
as the seas shall rise and fall

at the bidding of Our Lady;
as the sands of time shall pass and repass;
ever round and on; so, then, be it thus:
that the poison in the body shall issue forth
flowing ever away, to return from whence it came.
Back it shall go to its sender,
gaining in strength and malefic power
'till, reaching the would-be tormentor, it strikes
with three-fold the effect with which it came!
So mote it be; ever thus and anon.

Extinguish the black and brown candles, then sit for five minutes with thoughts of new power and strength flowing into the petitioner's mind and body. See the petitioner revitalized; uncrossed. After five minutes thus, extinguish the remaining candles.

The ritual should be repeated every three days, moving the two black candles an inch or so outward from the petitioner each time. Continue until the black candles finally reach and touch the brown ones.

⚜ UNDERSTANDING ⚜

ALTAR 1   FIGURE   ALTAR 2

CENSER

LIGHT BLUE 1

LIGHT BLUE 3   PETITIONER   LIGHT BLUE 4

LIGHT BLUE 2

BOOK

To Develop Understanding

Light altar candles 1 and 2.

Light incense, which should preferably be mixed with a little cinnamon and mastic.

Light petitioner's candle, concentrating your thoughts on petitioner. Light light blue candles 1, 2, 3, and 4, while thinking hard on the need to have understanding of other people; to see their point of view; to be sympathetic.

Then quietly say:

> Soars he on high the eagle
> aloft his eyes see down;
> would he were mouse, or rabbit, hare,
> to sense th'impending doom.
> Each to the other thinking not
> yet turned all 'bout would care a jot.

> To chase the doe the hounds spring forth
> so fleet and swift and fey.
> Yet swung about they'd feel death's teeth
> snap at their heels this day.
> Each to the other thinking not
> yet turned all 'bout would care a jot.

> Lamb to the wolf doth simply fall,
> it struggles not for fear;
> but should the wolf be prey'd upon
> by lamb, then howls would hear.
> Each to the other thinking not
> yet turned all 'bout would care a jot.

> Let not that I should be unthinking,
> uncaring; lacking feeling, sensing.
> Let not that I should see but one way
> not returning.
> Make me receive what I am giving,
> that understanding is within me.

Sit quietly for ten minutes before extinguishing the candles.

Repeat ritual every night for seven nights.

Part Two

Christian Rituals

AFFAIR

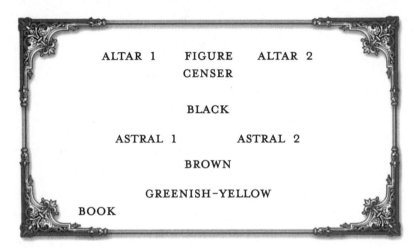

ALTAR 1   FIGURE   ALTAR 2
CENSER

BLACK

ASTRAL 1   ASTRAL 2

BROWN

GREENISH-YELLOW

BOOK

To Break Up a Love Affair

Light altar candles 1 and 2.

Light incense.

Light black candle, thinking of the love affair breaking up.

Light astral 1 (astral colors of the man in the affair) while thinking of the man.

Light astral 2 (astral colors of the woman in the affair) while thinking of the woman.

Light the brown candle, thinking of the love between the two slowly dying out; doubts and tension between them.

Light greenish-yellow, thinking of them being angry with each other; jealous of each other; general discord between the two.

Then say:

(PSALM 3)

O Lord, how are my foes increas'd?
Against me many rise.
Many say of my soul, For him
in God no succour lies.
Yet thou my shield and glory art,
th'uplifter of mine head.
I cry'd, and, from his holy hill,
the Lord me answer made.
I laid me down and slept, I wak'd,
for God sustained me.
I will not fear though thousands ten
set round against me be.
Arise, O Lord; save me, my God;
for thou my foes hast stroke
All on the cheek-bone, and the teeth
of wicked men hast broke.
Salvation doth appertain
unto the Lord alone:
Thy blessing, Lord, for evermore
thy people is upon.

Sit and concentrate on the love affair breaking up and the two people going their separate ways.

After approximately ten minutes of such concentration, extinguish the candles.

Repeat the ritual every Saturday, each time moving the two astral candles an inch or so further apart. Continue until they are finally at the far edges of the altar.

AMULET

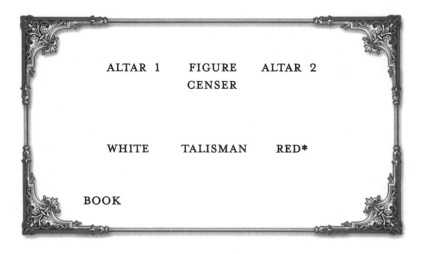

ALTAR 1   FIGURE   ALTAR 2
           CENSER

WHITE   TALISMAN   RED*

BOOK

Consecration of an
Amulet or Talisman

This ritual is for the consecration of a talisman, an amulet, or a "good luck charm." The talisman may be one that was made for you by someone else, or one that you made yourself. The latter is preferable.

Light altar candles 1 and 2.

Light incense (frankincense recommended).

Light white candle and say:

Here burns the sincerity of . . . (petitioner's name) . . . ,
his/her belief in the power of the talisman burns
as strongly as does this flame. It will never die.

Light red* candle and say:

Here is the love that goes into the talisman.*
For the talisman is a storehouse
of the power of love.

Take up the talisman and, holding it by the edge, pass it three times through the flame of the white candle, turning it over so that both sides are touched by the flame. (Don't burn your fingers!) Say:

By fire do I cleanse this talisman of any and
all impurities that may dwell within it.

Now pass it three times through the smoke of the incense, saying:

And by the power of God
I cense and cleanse it to be ready for my purpose.

Now take the talisman and hold it firmly in your right hand (left hand if left-handed) and say:

This talisman I imbue with love.
Whoever shall wear it shall feel that awesome power.
That power will be ever with its wearer,
so long as he/she shall bear it.

---

* The color and purpose of this candle will depend upon the purpose of the talisman (i.e., red for love; blue for health; green for fertility, etc.)

Now pass the talisman three times through the flame of the red candle. Say:

Here is that love, fully consecrated within.

Lay the talisman between the white and red candles. Extinguish the flames.

Let the talisman remain undisturbed for three hours. It should then be carried, or worn, by its owner, preferably worn next to the skin.

BAD HABIT

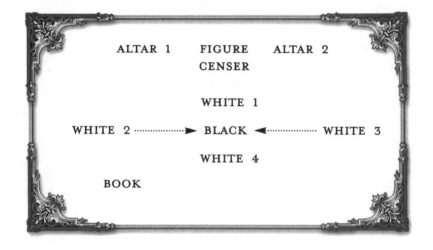

ALTAR 1   FIGURE   ALTAR 2
CENSER

WHITE 1

WHITE 2 ·········► BLACK ◄········· WHITE 3

WHITE 4

BOOK

To Overcome a Bad Habit

Light altar candles 1 and 2.

Light incense.

Light black candle and think of the bad habit to be overcome.

Light white candles 1, 2, 3, and 4, thinking of the bad habit fading away and finally being defeated. Say:

(PSALM 26)

Judge me, O Lord, for I have walk'd
in mine integrity:
I trusted also in the Lord;
slide therefore shall not I.
Examine me, and do me prove;
try heart and reins, O God:
For thy love is before mine eyes,
thy truth's path I have trod.
With persons vain I have not sat,
nor with dissemblers gone:
Th'assembly of ill men I hate;
to sit with such I shun.
Mine hands in innocence, O Lord,
I'll wash and purify;
So to thine holy altar go,
and compass it will I:
That I, with voice of thanksgiving,
may publish and declare,
And tell of all thy mighty works,
that great and wondrous are.
The habitation of thy house, Lord,
I have loved well;
Yea, in that place I do delight
where doth thine honour dwell.
With sinners gather not my soul,
and such as blood would spill:

Whose hands mischievous plots,
right hand corrupting bribes do fill.
But as for me, I will walk on
in mine integrity:
Do thou redeem me, and, O Lord,
be merciful to me.
My foot upon an even place
doth stand with steadfastness:
Within the congregations
th'Eternal I will bless.

Sit for fifteen minutes before extinguishing the candles; black first.

Repeat the ritual at the same time every week, each time moving white candles 2 and 3 a few inches in toward the black candle. Continue weekly until the white candles touch the black.

CONDITIONS

```
     ALTAR 1      FIGURE     ALTAR 2
                  CENSER


                   PINK

                PETITIONER

  LIGHT BLUE               ORANGE


   BOOK
```

To Settle a Disturbed Condition in the Home

Light altar candles 1 and 2.

Light incense.

Meditate on what is to be done.

Light petitioner's candle, thinking hard about petitioner.

Light light blue, pink, and orange candles, in that order, thinking of peace and tranquility within the home in question.

Meditate for a moment, then say:

(PSALM 1)

That man hath perfect blessedness who walketh not astray
In counsel of ungodly men, nor stands in sinners' way,
Nor sitteth in the scorner's chair: but placeth his delight
Upon God's law, and meditates on his law day and night.
He shall be like a tree that grows near planted by a river,
Which in his season yields his fruit, and his leaf fadeth never:
And all he doth shall prosper well. The wicked are not so;
But like they are unto the chaff, which wind drives to and fro.
In judgement therefore shall not stand such as ungodly are;
Now in th'assembly of the just shall wicked men appear.
For why? The way of godly men unto the Lord is known:
Whereas the way of wicked men shall quite be overthrown.

The candles are allowed to burn for fifteen minutes, during which time the above psalm is read and reread. At the end of that time the flames may be extinguished.

This ritual should be repeated on three consecutive nights.

```
ALTAR 1      FIGURE      ALTAR 2
             CENSER

             LIGHT BLUE

             ASTRAL

             PHOTO

BOOK
```

For the Dead

(*Note:* In this ritual a photograph of the deceased may be placed before his or her astral candle.)

Light altar candles 1 and 2.

Light incense.

Light astral candle of the deceased, thinking of him or her as you knew best.

Light light blue candle, thinking of peace and tranquility. Say:

(THE SONG OF SOLOMON, CH. 2)

I am the rose of Sharon, and the lily of the valleys.
As the lily among thorns, so is my love among the daughters.
As the apple-tree among the trees of the wood,
so is my beloved among the sons.
I sat down under his shadow with great delight,
and his fruit was sweet to my taste.
He brought me to the banqueting house,
and his banner over me was love.
His left hand is under my head,
and his right hand doth embrace me.
I charge you, O ye daughters of Jerusalem,
by the roes, and by the hinds of the field, that ye stir not up,
nor awake my love, till he please.
The voice of my beloved! Behold,
he cometh leaping upon the mountains,
skipping upon the hills.
My beloved is like a roe, or a young hart:
behold, he standeth behind our wall,
he looketh forth at the windows,
shewing himself through the lattice.
My beloved spake, and said unto me,
Rise up, my love, my fair one, and come away.
For, lo, the winter is past, the rain is over and gone;
The flowers appear on the earth;
the time of the singing of birds is come,
and the voice of the turtle is heard in our land;
The fig-tree putteth forth her green figs,

and the vines with the tender grape give a good smell.
Arise, my love, my fair one, and come away.
O my dove, that art in the clefts of the rock,
in the secret places of the stairs,
let me see thy countenance, let me hear thy voice;
for sweet is thy voice, and thy countenance is comely.
Take us the foxes, the little foxes, that spoil the vines:
for our vines have tender grapes.
My beloved is mine, and I am his;
he feedeth among the lilies.
Until the day break, and the shadows flee away,
turn, my beloved, and be thou like a roe or a young hart
upon the mountains of Bether.

Let the candles burn for a half hour before extinguishing them. Repeat every night for at least nine nights—longer if desired.

It is possible to obtain very large long-burning candles and these should, if possible, be used for the astral and light blue candles in this ritual.

DREAMS

ALTAR 1   FIGURE   ALTAR 2
             CENSER

LIGHT BLUE   WHITE

PETITIONER

ORANGE

BOOK   DAY
                      CANDLE

To Cause Dreams

Light altar candles 1 and 2.

Light incense.

Light petitioner's candle, thinking of petitioner.

Light light blue candle, thinking of peace and tranquility.

Light orange candle, thinking of what it is you wish to dream about.

Light white candle, thinking of truth in your dreams. Say:

(PSALM 11)

I in the Lord to put my trust;
how is it then that ye
Say to my soul, Flee, as a bird,
unto your mountain high?

For, lo, the wicked bend their bow,
their shafts on string they fit,
That those who upright are in heart
they privily may hit.
If the foundations be destroy'd,
what hath the righteous done?

God in his holy temple is,
in heaven is his throne:
His eyes do see, his eyelids try
men's sons. The just he proves:
But his soul hates the wicked man,
and him that vi'lence loves.

Snares, fire and brimstone, furious storms,
on sinners he shall rain:
This, as the portion of their cup,
doth unto them pertain.

Because the Lord most righteous doth
in righteousness delight;
And with pleasant countenance
beholdeth the upright.

Sit quietly for a few minutes before extinguishing the candles. This ritual should be performed at night, before going to bed, when dreams are desired.

ENEVY

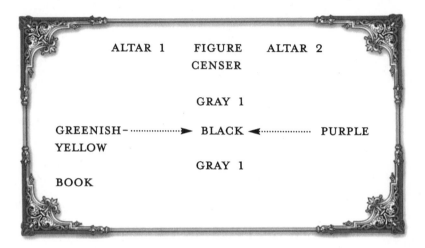

ALTAR 1   FIGURE   ALTAR 2
CENSER

GRAY 1

GREENISH- ········▶ BLACK ◄········ PURPLE
YELLOW

GRAY 1

BOOK

To Bring Pressure to Bear on an Enemy

Light altar candles 1 and 2.

Light incense.

Light black candle, thinking of enemy.

Light gray 1 and 2, thinking of frustration, stalemate.

Light greenish-yellow, thinking of anger, discord, sickness, and fright.

Light purple, thinking of tension, nervousness.

Think for a moment of your enemy feeling completely alone; unsure of himself/herself; nervous and frightened. Then say:

(PSALM 70)

Make haste, O God, me to preserve;
with speed, Lord, succour me.
Let them that for my soul do seek
sham'd and confounded be:
Let them be turned back, and sham'd
that in my hurt delight.
Turn'd back be they, Ha, ha! that say,
their shaming to requite.
O Lord, in thee let all be glad,
and joy that seek for thee:
Let them who thy salvation love
say still, God praised be.
But I both poor and needy am;
come, Lord, and make no stay:
My help thou and deliv'rer art;
O Lord, make no delay.

Blow out the black candle.

Sit for a moment thinking of your enemy confused.

Then relight it and say:

Make haste, O God, me to preserve;
with speed, Lord, succour me.

Let them that for my soul do seek
sham'd and confounded be:
Let them be turned back, and sham'd
that in my hurt delight.
Turn'd back be they, Ha, ha! that say,
their shaming to requite.
O Lord, in thee let all be glad,
and joy that seek for thee:
Let them who thy salvation love
say still, God praised be.
But I both poor and needy am;
come, Lord, and make no stay:
My help thou and deliv'rer art;
O Lord, make no delay.

Again sit thinking of your enemy thoroughly confused.

Repeat the following night, moving the greenish-yellow and purple candles two inches in toward the center. Repeat nightly till they touch.

EVIL

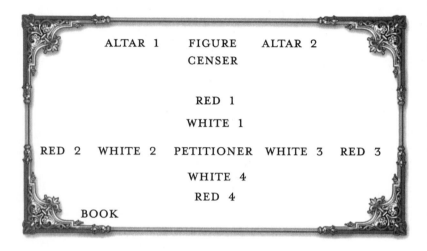

ALTAR 1   FIGURE   ALTAR 2
CENSER

RED 1

WHITE 1

RED 2   WHITE 2   PETITIONER   WHITE 3   RED 3

WHITE 4

RED 4

BOOK

To Protect against Evil

To "Uncross" a Person

Light altar candles 1 and 2.

Light incense, preferably frankincense.

Light petitioner's candle whilst picturing petitioner dressed all in white.

Light white candles 1, 2, 3, and 4, thinking of purity and truth.

Light red candles 1, 2, 3, and 4, thinking of strength to overcome evil, and of health and power. Then say:

(PSALM 93)

The Lord doth reign, and cloth'd is he
with majesty most bright;
His works do shew him cloth'd to be,
and girt about with might.
The world is also stablished,
that it cannot depart.
Thy throne is fix'd of old, and thou
from everlasting art.
The floods, O Lord, have lifted up,
they lifted up their voice;
the floods have lifted up their waves,
and made a mighty noise.
But yet the Lord, that is on high,
is more of might by far
than noise of many waters is,
or great sea-billows are.
Thy testimonies ev'ry one
in faithfulness excel;
and holiness for ever, Lord,
thine house becometh well.

Let the candles burn right down until they go out.

FEAR

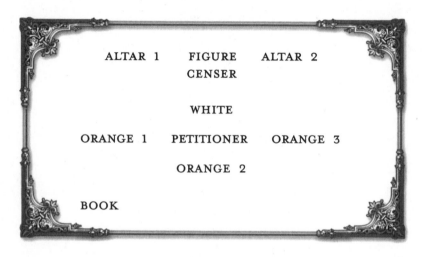

ALTAR 1   FIGURE   ALTAR 2
            CENSER

            WHITE

ORANGE 1   PETITIONER   ORANGE 3

            ORANGE 2

BOOK

To Conquer Fear

Light altar candles 1 and 2.

Light incense.

Concentrate on conquering fear.

Light petitioner's candle while thinking of petitioner.

Light white candle while thinking of strength and purity.

Light orange candles 1, 2, and 3 while thinking of self-confidence, ability to overcome fear, and strength of personality.

Meditate a moment, then say:

(PSALM 31)

In thee O Lord, I put my trust,
sham'd let me never be;
According to thy righteousness do thou deliver me.
Bow down thy ear to me,
with speed send me deliverance:
To save me, my strong rock be thou,
and my house of defence.
Because thou art my rock,
and thee I for my fortress take;
Therefore do thou me lead and guide,
ev'n for thine own name's sake.
And sith thou art my strength,
therefore pull me out of the net,
which they in subtilty for me so privily have set.
Into thine hands I do commit my sp'rit:
for thou art he,
O thou, JEHOVAH, God of truth,
that hast redeemed me.
Those that do lying vanities regard,
I have abhorr'd:
But as for me, my confidence is fixed on the Lord.
I'll in thy mercy gladly joy:

for thou thy miseries
Consider'd hast;
thou hast my soul known in adversities:
And thou hast not inclosed me
within the en'my's hand;
And by thee have my feet been made
in a large room to stand.
O Lord, upon me mercy have, for trouble is on me:
Mine eye, my belly, and my soul,
with grief consumed be.
Because my life with grief is spent,
my years with sighs and groans:

My strength doth fail;
and for my skin consumed are my bones.
I was a scorn to all my foes,
and to my friends a fear;
And specially reproach'd of those
that were my neighbours near.
When they me saw they from me fled.
Ev'n so I am forgot,
as men are out of mind when dead:
I'm like a broken pot.
For slanders I of many heard;
fear compass'd me, while they against me did consult,
and plot to take my life away.
But as for me, O Lord, my trust upon thee I did lay;
And I to thee, thou art my God,
did confidently say.

My times are wholly in thine hand:
do thou deliver me
From their hands that mine enemies
and persecutors be.
Thy countenance to shine
do thou upon thy servant make:
Unto me give salvation,
for thy great mercies' sake.
Let me not be asham'd, O Lord,
for on thee call'd I have:
Let wicked men be sham'd,
let them be silent in the grave.
To silence put the lying lips,
that grievous things do say,
and hard reports, in pride and scorn,
on righteous men do lay.
How great's the goodness thou for them
that fear thee keep'st in store,
and wrought'st for them that trust in thee
the sons of men before.
In secret of thy presence
thou shalt hide them from man's pride:
From strife of tongues thou closely shalt,
as in a tent, them hide.
All praise and thanks be to the Lord:
for he hath magnify'd
His wondrous love to me
within a city fortify'd.

For from thine eyes cut off I am,
I in my haste had said;
My voice yet heard'st thou,
when to thee with cries my moan I made.
O love the Lord, all ye his saints;
because the Lord doth guard the faithful,
and he plenteously proud doers doth reward.
Be of good courage,
and he strength unto your heart shall send,
all ye whose hope and confidence
doth on the Lord depend.

Sit for five minutes in meditation, then extinguish the flames.

Repeat every night for nine nights.

HAPPINESS

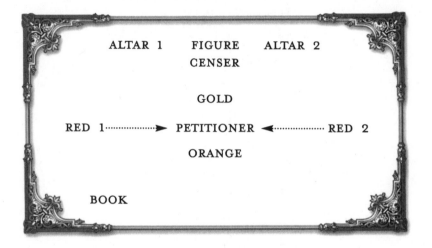

ALTAR 1   FIGURE   ALTAR 2
CENSER

GOLD

RED 1 ············▶ PETITIONER ◀············ RED 2

ORANGE

BOOK

To Win or Hold Happiness

Light altar candles 1 and 2.

Light incense.

Light petitioner's candle, thinking of petitioner.

Light gold candle and orange candle, thinking of the petitioner attracting happiness to herself or himself. Light red candles 1 and 2, thinking of all the happiness that petitioner desires and deserves.

Think of all this happiness flowing in to the petitioner. Then say:

(PSALM 11)

I in the Lord do put my trust;
how is it then that ye
Say to my soul, Flee, as a bird,
unto your mountain high?

For, lo, the wicked bend their bow,
their shafts on string they fit,
That those who upright are in heart
they privily may hit.
If the foundations be destroy'd,
What hath the righteous done?

God in his holy temple is,
in heaven is his throne:
His eyes do see, his eyelids try
men's sons. The just he proves:
But his soul hates the wicked man,
and him that vi'lence loves.

Snares, fire and brimstone, furious storms,
on sinners he shall rain:
This, as the portion of their cup,
doth unto them pertain.

Because the Lord most righteous doth
in righteousness delight;

And with a pleasant countenance
beholdeth the upright.

Sit for fifteen minutes thinking of the happiness
which is the petitioner's. Then extinguish the candles. Repeat the ritual successive nights, each time
moving the red candles two inches in toward the
petitioner. Continue until the two red candles actually touch the petitioner.

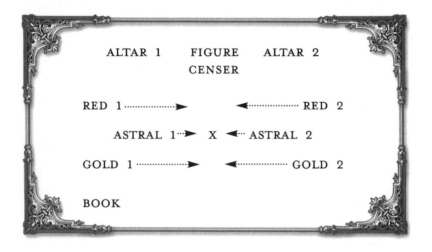

```
        ALTAR 1      FIGURE      ALTAR 2
                     CENSER

   RED  1 ·················▶        ◀················· RED  2

        ASTRAL 1···▶  X  ◀··· ASTRAL  2

   GOLD  1 ·················▶     ◀················· GOLD  2


   BOOK
```

To Heal an Unhappy Marriage

Light altar candles 1 and 2.

Light incense.

Meditate on what is to be done.

Light astral 1, red 1, gold 1 while thinking of the husband.

Light astral 2, red 2, gold 2 while thinking of the wife. Say:

(SONG OF SOLOMON, CH. 3)

By night on my bed I sought him whom my soul loveth:
I sought him, but I found him not.
I will rise now, and go about the city in the streets,
and in the broad ways I will seek him whom my soul loveth:
I sought him but I found him not.
The watchmen that go about the city found me:
to whom I said, "Saw ye him whom my soul loveth?"
It was but a little that I passed from them,
but I found him whom my soul loveth:
I held him, and would not let him go,
until I had brought him into my mother's house,
and into the chamber of her that conceived me.
I charge you, O ye daughters of Jerusalem,
by the roes, and by the hinds of the field,
that ye stir not up, nor awake my love, till he please.
Who is this that cometh out of the wilderness
like pillars of smoke, perfumed with myrrh and frankincense,
with all the powders of the merchant?
Behold his bed, which is Solomon's;
threescore valiant men are about it,
of the valiant of Israel.
They all hold swords being expert in war:
every man hath his sword upon his thigh,
because of fear in the night.
King Solomon made himself a chariot
of the wood of Lebanon.

He made the pillars thereof of silver,
the bottom thereof of gold, the covering of it of purple,
the midst thereof being paved with love,
for the daughters of Jerusalem.
Go forth, O ye daughters of Zion,
and behold King Solomon with the crown
wherewith his mother crowned him
in the day of his espousals,
and in the day of the gladness of his heart.

Repeat ritual alternate nights for nine days; each time moving the two groups of candles one inch closer to each other.

HEALTH

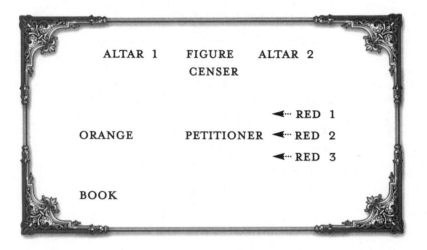

ALTAR 1	FIGURE	ALTAR 2
	CENSER	
		◄··· RED 1
ORANGE	PETITIONER ◄···	RED 2
		◄··· RED 3
BOOK		

To Regain (or Retain) Good Health

Light altar candles 1 and 2.

Light incense.

Light petitioner's candle, picturing petitioner.

Light orange candle, thinking of encouragement and attraction.

Light red candles 1, 2, and 3, thinking of strength and health.

Think of all the strength and health flowing into the petitioner as you say:

(PSALM 23)

The Lord's my shepherd, I'll not want.
He makes me down to lie
In pastures green: he leadeth me
The quiet waters by.
My soul he doth restore again;
And me to walk doth make
Within the paths of righteousness,
Ev'n for his own name's sake.
Yea, though I walk in death's dark vale,
Yet will I fear none ill:
For thou art with me; and thy rod
And staff me comfort still.
My table thou hast furnished
In presence of my foes,
My head thou dost with oil anoint,
And my cup overflows.
Goodness and mercy all my life
Shall surely follow me:
And in God's house for evermore
My dwelling-place shall be.

Sit quietly meditating on the wonderful good health enjoyed, and to be enjoyed, by the petitioner. Sit thus for ten to fifteen minutes, then extinguish the candles. Repeat this ritual every Friday evening for seven Fridays, each time moving the three red candles a little closer in toward the petitioner. On the seventh Friday they should touch.

JEALOUSY

ALTAR 1	FIGURE	ALTAR 2
	CENSER	

BROWN 1	GREENISH-YELLOW 1
	ASTRAL

GREENISH-YELLOW 2	BROWN 2

BOOK

To Arouse Jealousy

Light altar candles 1 and 2.

Light incense.

Light astral candle of the person in whom it is desired to arouse jealousy. Think hard of him or her. Light brown candles 1 and 2, thinking of uncertainty, hesitation.

Light greenish-yellow candles 1 and 2, thinking of sickness, jealousy, and discord. Then say:

(PSALM 63)

Lord, thee my God, I'll early seek:
My soul doth thirst for thee;
my flesh longs in a dry parch'd land,
Wherein no waters be:
That I thy power may behold,
and brightness of thy face,
As I have seen thee heretofore
within thy holy place.
Since better is thy love than life,
my lips thee praise shall give.
I in thy name will lift my hands,
and bless thee while I live.
Ev'n as with marrow and with fat
my soul shall filled be:
Then shall my mouth with joyful lips
sing praises unto thee:
When I do thee upon my bed
remember with delight,
and when on thee I meditate
in watches of the night.
In shadow of thy wings I'll joy;
for thou mine help hast been.
My soul thee follows hard; and me
thy right hand doth sustain.
Who seek my soul to spill shall sink
down to earth's lowest room.

They by the sword shall be cut off,
and foxes' prey become.
Yet shall the king in God rejoice,
and each one glory
shall that swear by him:
but stopp'd shall be
the mouth of liars all.

Extinguish all candles.

Perform ritual every Monday and Saturday for three weeks.

LOVE

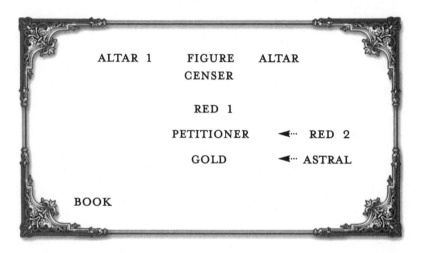

```
ALTAR 1        FIGURE      ALTAR
               CENSER

               RED  1
           PETITIONER      ◄··· RED  2
             GOLD          ◄··· ASTRAL

BOOK
```

To Win the Love of
a Man or a Woman

Light altar candles 1 and 2.

Light incense.

Meditate.

Light petitioner's candle, thinking of him or her.

Light red 1 thinking of petitioner's love and strength.

Light gold thinking of great attraction petitioner has; how he or she draws people to him or her.

Light astral candle for the one petitioner wishes to win, thinking of him or her and picturing him or her.

Light red 2 thinking of that person's love for the petitioner. If petitioner is male, the practitioner should then say:

(SONG OF SOLOMON, CH. 6)

Whither is thy beloved gone,
O thou fairest among women?
Whither is thy beloved turned aside?
that we may seek him from thee.
My beloved is gone down into his garden,
to the beds of spices,
to feed in the gardens, and to gather lilies.
I am my beloved's, and my beloved is mine;
he feedeth among the lilies.
Thou art beautiful, O my love, as Tirzah,
comely as Jerusalem, terrible as an army with banners.
Turn away thine eyes from me, for they have overcome me:
thy hair is as a flock of goats that appear from Gilead:
Thy teeth are as a flock of sheep
which go up from the washing,
whereof every one beareth twins,
and there is not one barren among them.
As a piece of pomegranate are thy temples within thy locks.
There are threescore queens,
and fourscore concubines,

and virgins without number.
My dove, my undefiled is but one;
she is the only one of her mother,
she is the choice one of her that bare her:
the daughters saw her, and blessed her;
yea, the queens and the concubines,
and they praise her.
Who is she that looketh forth as the morning,
fair as the moon, clear as the sun,
and terrible as an army with banners?
I went down into the garden of nuts
to see the fruits of the valley,
and to see whether the vine flourished,
and the pomegranates budded.
Or ever I was aware, my soul made me
like the chariots of Ammi-nadib.
Return, return, O Shulamite; return, return,
that we may look upon thee.
What will ye see in the Shulamite?
As it were the company of two armies.

If the petitioner is female then practitioner should say:

(SONG OF SOLOMON, CH. 8)
Oh that thou wert as my brother,
that sucked the breasts of my mother!
When I should find thee without, I would kiss thee;
yea, I should not be despised.

I would lead thee, and bring thee into my mother's house,
who would instruct me:
I would cause thee to drink of spiced wine
of the juice of my pomegranate.
His left hand should be under my head,
and his right hand should embrace me.
I charge you, O daughters of Jerusalem,
that ye stir not up, nor awake my love, until he please.
Who is this that cometh up from the wilderness
leaning upon her beloved?
I raise thee up under the apple-tree:
there thy mother brought thee forth;
there she brought thee forth that bare thee.
Set me as a seal upon thy heart,
as a seal upon thine arm:
for love is strong as death;
jealousy as cruel as the grave:
the coals thereof are coals of fire,
which hath a most vehement flame.
Many waters cannot quench love,
neither can the floods drown it:
if a man would give all the substance of his house for love,
it would utterly be contemned.
We have a little sister, and she hath no breasts:
What shall we do for our sister in the day
when she shall be spoken for?
If she be a wall, we will build upon her a palace of silver;

and if she be a door, we will inclose her with boards of cedar.
I am a wall, and my breasts like towers:
then was I in his eyes as one that found favor.
Solomon had a vineyard at Baal-hamon;
he let out the vineyard unto keepers:
every one for the fruit thereof was to bring
a thousand pieces of silver.
My vineyard, which is mine, is before me:
thou, O Solomon, must have a thousand,
and those that keep the fruit thereof two hundred.
Thou that dwellest in the gardens,
the companions hearken to thy voice;
cause me to hear it.
Make haste, my beloved,
and be thou like to a roe or to a young hart
upon the mountains of spices.

Repeat the ritual the following day after moving red 2 and the astral one inch to the left. Continue daily until red 2 and the astral touch the petitioner's candle.

LUCK

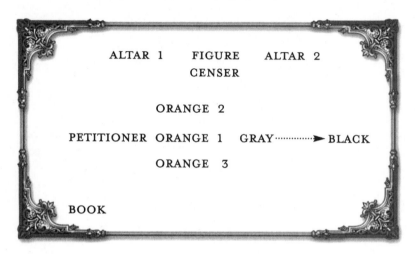

ALTAR 1   FIGURE   ALTAR 2
CENSER

ORANGE 2

PETITIONER ORANGE 1   GRAY ·········➤ BLACK

ORANGE 3

BOOK

To Change One's Luck

Light altar candles 1 and 2. Light incense.

Light petitioner's candle, picturing petitioner. Light orange 1, 2 and 3, thinking of encouraging petitioner; of petitioner's luck changing, changing for the better. Light black candle, thinking of the bad luck that is going to disappear.

Light gray candle, thinking of all bad luck being cancelled out; neutralized, before changing to good luck.

Then say:

(PSALM 62: VERSES 3, 4, 11, 12)

How long will ye
against a man plot mischief? Ye shall all
Be slain; ye as a tott'ring fence shall be,
and bowing wall.
They only plot to cast him down from his excellency:
They joy in lies; with mouth they bless,
but they curse inwardly.

God hath it spoken once to me, yea, this I heard again,
that power to almighty God alone doth appertain.
Yea, mercy also unto thee belongs, O Lord, alone:
For thou according to his work rewardest ev'ry one.

Blow out the black candle; sit for a moment, then
relight it. Say again:

How long will ye
against a man plot mischief? Ye shall all
Be slain; ye as a tott'ring fence shall be,
and bowing wall.
They only plot to cast him down from his excellency:
They joy in lies; with mouth they bless,
but they curse inwardly.

God hath it spoken once to me, yea, this I heard again,
that power to almighty God alone doth appertain.
Yea, mercy also unto thee belongs, O Lord, alone:
For thou according to his work rewardest ev'ry one.

Blow out the black candle; sit for a moment, then relight it. Say again:

> *How long will ye*
> *against a man plot mischief? Ye shall all*
> *Be slain; ye as a tott'ring fence shall be,*
> *and bowing wall.*
> *They only plot to cast him down from his excellency:*
> *They joy in lies; with mouth they bless,*
> *but they curse inwardly.*

> *God hath it spoken once to me, yea, this I heard again,*
> *that power to almighty God alone doth appertain.*
> *Yea, mercy also unto thee belongs, O Lord, alone:*
> *For thou according to his work rewardest ev'ry one.*

Concentrate on the petitioner's luck changing from bad to good.

Extinguish the candles.

Repeat the ritual successive nights, each time moving the gray candle one inch toward the black. Continue until they meet.

MEDITATION

```
        ALTAR  1      FIGURE      ALTAR  2
                      CENSER


 LIGHT BLUE 1        PETITIONER/     LIGHT BLUE 2
                     MEDITATOR


      BOOK                      DAY CANDLE
```

To Meditate

Light altar candles 1 and 2.

Light day candle.

Light incense.

Light petitioner's candle, thinking of petitioner.

Light light blue candles, thinking of peace and tranquility. Say:

We have found thee in the order of nature
and in the workings of history.
But we have not known thee as we should in our lives.
Yet thou art not far from us,
and it is our own mistake
when we work for even a single day
Without thy gracious companionship.
Aid us, we beseech thee, to make real to ourselves
thy presence and thy help.
May no cloud obscure thy face,
but may the light of thy glory guide us all our way of life.
Make this day one of joy and growth to us,
and may the evening find us nearer the goal
to which we take our way.
Help us to understand the wealth thou hast committed
to us in the rare fruits and flowers that may bloom
in the gardens of our souls.
May we spare no effort in their care,
even as we labor for material good.
Come and counsel us in the high tillage of our lives.
And may the ingathering at the last be for
our own enrichment and for thy approval.

Settle into your preferred meditation style (i.e., transcendental, mantric-yogic, etc.).

At the end of meditation, extinguish candles, reversing the order of lighting.

MONEY

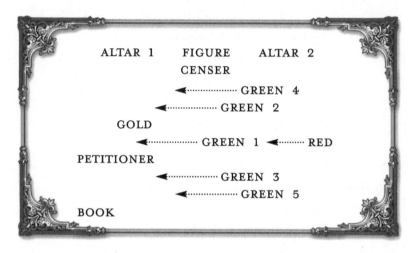

```
ALTAR 1      FIGURE      ALTAR 2
                CENSER
                ◄·············· GREEN  4
                ◄·············· GREEN  2
        GOLD
            ◄·············· GREEN  1 ◄········ RED
PETITIONER
            ◄·············· GREEN  3
            ◄·············· GREEN  5
BOOK
```

To Obtain Money

Light altar candles 1 and 2.

Light incense.

Meditate on what is to be done.

Light petitioner's candle, picturing petitioner.

Light gold, thinking "attraction."

Light greens, in order noted, thinking "money."

Light red, thinking of what is to be accomplished.

Meditate for a moment or two, then say:

(PSALM 41)

Blessed is he that wisely doth The poor man's case consider;
For when the time of trouble is, the Lord will them deliver.
God will keep him, yea, save alive; on earth he bless'd shall live;
And to his enemies' desire thou wilt not up him give.
God will give strength when he on bed of languishing doth mourn;
And in his sickness sore, O Lord, thou all his bed wilt turn.
I said, O Lord, do thou extend thy mercy unto me;
O do thou heal my soul; for why? I have offended thee.
Those that to me are enemies, of me do evil say,
when shall he die, that so his name may perish quite away?
To see me if he comes, he speaks vain words; but then his heart
Heaps mischief to it, which he tells, when forth he doth depart.
My haters jointly whispering 'gainst me my hurt devise.
Mischief, say they, cleaves fast to him he li'th, and shall not rise.
Yea, ev'n mine own familiar friend, on whom I did rely,
Who ate my bread, ev'n he his heel against me lifted high.
But, Lord, be merciful to me, and up again me raise,
that I may justly them requite according to their ways.
By this I know that certainly I favour'd am by thee;
Because my fateful enemy triumphs not over me.
But as for me, thou me uphold'st in mine integrity;
And me before thy countenance thou sett'st continually.
The Lord, the God of Israel, be bless'd for ever then,
from age to age eternally. Amen, yea, and amen.

An alternative to the above is the Twenty-third
Psalm:

The Lord's my shepherd, I'll not want.
He makes me down to lie
In pastures green: he leadeth me
The quiet waters by.
My soul he doth restore again;
And me to walk doth make
Within the paths of righteousness,
Ev'n for his own name's sake.
Yea, though I walk in death's dark vale,
Yet will I fear none ill:
For thou art with me; and thy rod
And staff me comfort still.
My table thou hast furnished
In presence of my foes,
My head thou dost with oil anoint,
And my cup overflows.
Goodness and mercy all my life
Shall surely follow me:
And in God's house for evermore
My dwelling-place shall be.

Repeat the ritual the following day, after moving the
green and the red candles two inches to the left. Continue daily until green 1 touches gold and petitioner.

ALTAR 1   FIGURE   ALTAR 2
CENSER

ORANGE

PETITIONER

LIGHT BLUE 1   LIGHT BLUE 2

BOOK

To Soothe and Quiet the Nerves

Light altar candles 1 and 2.

Light incense.

Light petitioner's candle and concentrate on petitioner.

Light light blue candles 1 and 2 while thinking of peace and tranquility, patience and quiet satisfaction.

Light orange candle while thinking of stimulation, encouragement, and peace. Say:

(PSALM 37)

For evil-doers fret thou not thyself unquietly;
nor do thou envy bear to those that work iniquity.
For, even like unto the grass, soon be cut down shall they;
And, like the green and tender herb, they wither shall away.
Set thou thy trust upon the Lord, and be thou doing good;
And so thou in the land shalt dwell, and verily have food.
Delight thyself in God; he'll give thine heart's desire to thee.
Thy way to God commit, him trust, it bring to pass shall he.
And, like unto the light, he shall thy righteousness display;
And he thy judgement shall bring forth like noontide of the day.
Rest in the Lord, and patiently wait for him: do not fret
For him who, prosp'ring in his way, success in sin doth get.
Do thou from anger cease, and wrath see thou forsake also:
Fret not thyself in any wise, that evil thou should'st do.
For those that evil-doers are shall be cut off and fall:
But those that wait upon the Lord the earth inherit shall.
For yet a little while, and then the wicked shall not be;
His place thou shalt consider well, but it thou shalt not see.
But by inheritance the earth the meek ones shall possess:
They also shall delight themselves in an abundant peace.
The wicked plots against the just, and at him whets his teeth:
The Lord shall laugh at him, because his day he coming seeth.
The wicked have drawn out the sword,
and bent their bow, to slay
The poor and needy, and to kill men in an upright way.
But their own sword, which they have drawn,

shall enter their own heart;
Their bows which they have bent, shall break,
and into pieces part.
A little that a just man hath is more and better far
than is the wealth of many such as lewd and wicked are.
For sinners' arms shall broken be; just God the just sustains.
God knows the just man's days, and still their heritage remains.

Sit then quietly for fifteen minutes or so before extinguishing the flames. This ritual should be performed whenever you feel the need.

POWER

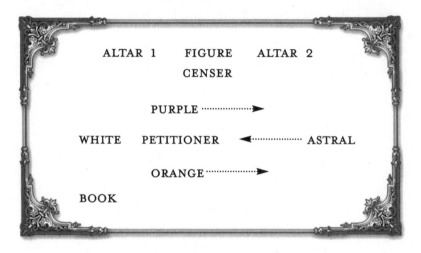

ALTAR 1   FIGURE   ALTAR 2

CENSER

PURPLE ·············▶

WHITE   PETITIONER   ◀············· ASTRAL

ORANGE ·············▶

BOOK

To Gain Power over Others

Light altar candles 1 and 2.

Light incense.

Light petitioner's candle, thinking of the petitioner. Light white candle, thinking of the strength of the petitioner.

Light astral candle of the person over whom petitioner wishes to gain power, thinking hard about that person.

Light purple candle, thinking of the power emanating from the petitioner, and how it can affect the other person.

Light orange candle, thinking of the attraction that petitioner has for the other person.

Then say:

(PSALM 130)

Lord, from the depths to thee I cry'd.
My voice, Lord, do thou hear:
Unto my supplication's voice
give an attentive ear.
Lord, who shall stand, if thou, O Lord,
should'st mark iniquity?
But yet with thee forgiveness is,
that fear'd thou mayest be.
I wait for God, my soul doth wait,
my hope is in his word.
More than they that for morning watch,
my soul waits for the Lord;
I say, more than they that do watch
the morning light to see.
Let Israel hope in the Lord,
for with him mercies be;
and plenteous redemption
is ever found with him.
And from all his iniquities
he Isr'el shall redeem.

Extinguish the candles.

Repeat every night for six nights. Each time move the astral candle one inch to the left (toward the center of the altar) and both the purple and orange candles one inch to the right (toward the center).

—❦ POWER INCREASE ❦—

```
        ALTAR  1      FIGURE       ALTAR  2
                      CENSER

                     PURPLE  1
    PURPLE  7                      PURPLE  2
                    PETITIONER
    PURPLE  6        GOLD          PURPLE  3
              PURPLE  5   PURPLE  4
        BOOK                               DAY
                                         CANDLE
```

To Increase Your Power*

Light altar candles 1 and 2.

Light incense.

Light petitioner's candle, thinking of petitioner.

Light gold candle, thinking of power being attracted to petitioner.

* Good for scrying powers, magickal powers, healing powers, ESP, etc.

Light day candle. (*Note:* This ritual should be started seven days before the full of the moon. The day candle is of the appropriate color for the ritual day [see table 2, page 11] and will therefore be a different candle each day the ritual is performed.)

Light purple candle 1, thinking of power—power to heal, or scry, or whatever the desire. (*Note:* On the second day of the ritual light purple candles 1 and 2; the third day, purple candles 1, 2, and 3; and so on.) Say:

(PSALM 127)

Except the Lord to build the house
the builders lose their pain.
Except the Lord the city keep,
and watchmen watch in vain.
'Tis vain for you to rise betimes,
or late from rest to keep,
To feed on sorrows' bread; so gives
he his beloved sleep.

Lo, children are God's heritage,
The womb's fruit his reward.
The sons of youth as arrows are,
For strong men's hands prepar'd.
O happy is the man that hath
his quiver fill'd with those;
They unashamed in the gate
Shall speak unto their foes.

Sit quietly for a while thinking of power building within the petitioner. Then say again:

Except the Lord to build the house,
the builders lose their pain,
Except the Lord the city keep,
and watchmen watch in vain.
'Tis vain for you to rise betimes,
or late from rest to keep,
To feed on sorrows' bread; so gives
he his beloved sleep.

Lo, children are God's heritage,
the womb's fruit his reward.
The sons of youth as arrows are,
for strong men's hands prepar'd.
O happy is the man that hath
his quiver fill'd with those;
They unashamed in the gate
shall speak unto their foes.

Extinguish the candles, reversing the order of lighting.

PROSPERITY

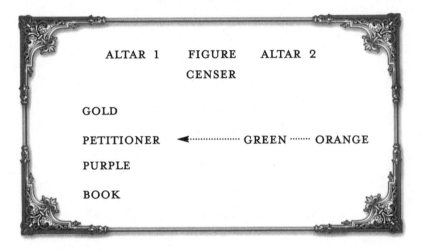

| ALTAR 1 | FIGURE | ALTAR 2 |
| | CENSER | |

GOLD

PETITIONER ◄·············· GREEN ······· ORANGE

PURPLE

BOOK

To Gain Prosperity

Light altar candles 1 and 2.

Light incense.

Light petitioner's candle while thinking of petitioner.

Light gold candle while thinking of attraction, confidence, and gain.

Light purple candle while thinking of progress and power.

Light green candle while thinking of money, wealth, and prosperity.

Light orange candle while thinking of the money and prosperity being attracted to the petitioner. Then say:

(PSALM 41)

Blessed is he that wisely doth The poor man's case consider;
For when the time of trouble is, the Lord will them deliver.
God will keep him, yea, save alive; on earth he bless'd shall live;
And to his enemies' desire thou wilt not up him give.
God will give strength when he on bed of languishing doth mourn;
And in his sickness sore, O Lord, thou all his bed wilt turn.
I said, O Lord, do thou extend thy mercy unto me;
O do thou heal my soul; for why? I have offended thee.
Those that to me are enemies, of me do evil say,
when shall he die, that so his name may perish quite away?
To see me if he comes, he speaks vain words; but then his heart
Heaps mischief to it, which he tells, when forth he doth depart.
My haters jointly whispering 'gainst me my hurt devise.
Mischief, say they, cleaves fast to him he li'th, and shall not rise.
Yea, ev'n mine own familiar friend, on whom I did rely,
Who ate my bread, ev'n he his heel against me lifted high.
But, Lord, be merciful to me, and up again me raise,
that I may justly them requite according to their ways.
By this I know that certainly I favour'd am by thee;
Because my fateful enemy triumphs not over me.
But as for me, thou me uphold'st in mine integrity;

And me before thy countenance thou sett'st continually.
The Lord, the God of Israel, be bless'd for ever then,
from age to age eternally. Amen, yea, and amen.

Sit for a moment before extinguishing candles. Repeat successive nights, each time moving the green and orange candles two inches to the left.

— ◆§ PURIFICATION §◆—

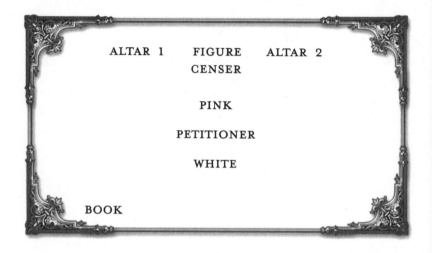

ALTAR 1   FIGURE   ALTAR 2
CENSER

PINK

PETITIONER

WHITE

BOOK

To Purify Oneself

Light altar candles 1 and 2.

Light incense.

Light petitioner's candle and think of petitioner.

Light pink candle and think of petitioner's honor, uprightness, and morality.

Light white candle and think of petitioner's sincerity, truth, and purity. Say:

(PSALM 23)

The Lord's my shepherd, I'll not want.
He makes me down to lie
In pastures green: he leadeth me
The quiet waters by.
My soul he doth restore again;
And me to walk doth make
Within the paths of righteousness,
Ev'n for his own name's sake.
Yea, though I walk in death's dark vale,
Yet will I fear none ill:
For thou art with me; and thy rod
And staff me comfort still.
My table thou hast furnished
In presence of my foes,
My head thou dost with oil anoint,
And my cup overflows.
Goodness and mercy all my life
Shall surely follow me:
And in God's house for evermore
My dwelling-place shall be.

Sit quietly for five minutes thinking of the purity
of the petitioner. Then say again:

The Lord's my shepherd, I'll not want.
He makes me down to lie
In pastures green: he leadeth me
The quiet waters by.

My soul he doth restore again;
And me to walk doth make
Within the paths of righteousness,
Ev'n for his own name's sake.
Yea, though I walk in death's dark vale,
Yet will I fear none ill:
For thou art with me; and thy rod
And staff me comfort still.
My table thou hast furnished
In presence of my foes,
My head thou dost with oil anoint,
And my cup overflows.
Goodness and mercy all my life
Shall surely follow me:
And in God's house for evermore
My dwelling-place shall be.

Sit quietly for five minutes thinking of the purity of the petitioner. Then repeat the psalm a third time.

After a further five minutes of contemplation, extinguish the candles.

Repeat every three days for as long as desired.

SCRYING

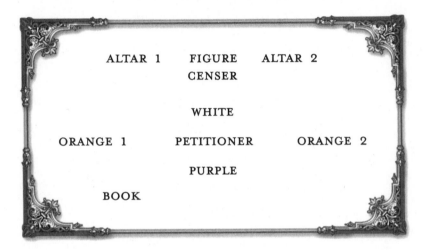

ALTAR 1	FIGURE	ALTAR 2
	CENSER	
	WHITE	
ORANGE 1	PETITIONER	ORANGE 2
	PURPLE	
BOOK		

For Scrying*

Light altar candles 1 and 2.

Light incense.

Light petitioner's candle and think of petitioner.

Light white candle, thinking of purity, truth, and sincerity.

Light purple candle, thinking of the power to divine, to scry.

* Equally suitable for crystal gazing, mirror gazing, or any other form of scrying art.

Light orange candles 1 and 2, thinking of that power being attracted to the petitioner. Say:

(PSALM 62)

My soul with expectation depends on God indeed:
My strength and my salvation
doth from him alone proceed.
He only my salvation is,
and my strong rock is he:
He only is my sure defence;
much mov'd I shall not be.

How long will ye against a man plot mischief? Ye shall all
Be slain;
ye as a tott'ring fence shall be, and bowing wall.
They only plot to cast him down from his excellency:
They joy in lies; with mouth they bless,
but they curse inwardly.

My soul wait thou with patience,
upon thy God alone;
On him dependeth all my hope and expectation.
He only my salvation is,
and my strong rock is he;
He only is my sure defence:
I shall not moved be.

In God my glory placed is,
and my salvation sure;
in God the rock is of my strength,
my refuge most secure.

Ye people, place your confidence in him continually;
Before him pour ye out your heart:
God is our refuge high.
God hath it spoken once to me,
yea, this I heard again,
That power to Almighty God alone doth appertain.
Yea, mercy also unto thee belongs,
O Lord, alone:
For thou according to his work rewardest ev'ryone.

Sit quietly for a few moments clearing your mind of everything. Then turn your back to the altar and gaze into the crystal. When you have accomplished what you wish, turn again to the altar and bow your head for a few moments in silence. Extinguish the candles.

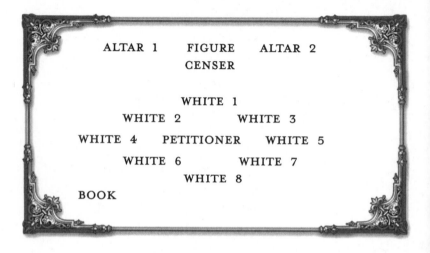

ALTAR 1   FIGURE   ALTAR 2
CENSER

WHITE 1

WHITE 2   WHITE 3

WHITE 4   PETITIONER   WHITE 5

WHITE 6   WHITE 7

WHITE 8

BOOK

To Stop Slander

Light altar candles I and 2. Light incense.

Light petitioner's candle whilst concentrating your thoughts on petitioner.

Light white candles I, 2, 3, 4, 5, 6, 7, and 8, and imagine the petitioner completely surrounded by purity, truth, and sincerity—an insurmountable barrier. Say:

(PSALM 2)

Why rage the heathen?
And vain things why do the people mind?
Kings of the earth do set themselves,
and princes are combin'd.
To plot against the Lord,
and his Anointed, saying thus,
Let us asunder break their bands,
and cast their cords from us.
He that in heaven sits shall laugh;
the Lord shall scorn them all.
Then shall he speak to them in wrath,
in rage he vex them shall.
Yet notwithstanding I have him to be my King appointed;
and over Sion, my holy hill,
I have him King anointed.
The sure decree I will declare;
the Lord hath said to me,
thou art mine only Son;
this day I have begotten thee.
Ask of me, and for heritage
the heathen I'll make thine;
And, for possession, I to thee
will give earth's utmost line.
Thou shalt, as with a weighty rod
of iron, break them all;
And, as a potter's sherd, thou shalt

them dash in pieces small.
Now therefore, kings, be wise; be taught,
ye judges of the earth:
Serve God in fear, and see that ye
join trembling with your mirth.
Kiss ye the Son, lest in his ire
ye perish from the way,
if once his wrath begin to burn:
bless'd all that on him stay.

Sit in quiet contemplation for ten minutes before extinguishing the candles.

Repeat this ritual every three nights for as long as desired.

SUCCESS

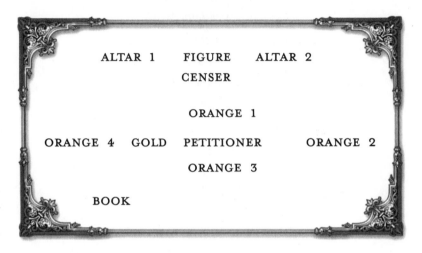

ALTAR 1		FIGURE	ALTAR 2
		CENSER	
		ORANGE 1	
ORANGE 4	GOLD	PETITIONER	ORANGE 2
		ORANGE 3	
BOOK			

To Attain Success

Light altar candles 1 and 2.

Light incense.

Light petitioner's candle, concentrating your thoughts on petitioner. Light gold candle and orange 1 (only), thinking of petitioner having great good luck in whatever petitioner endeavors. (See end of ritual for instructions concerning orange candles 2, 3, and 4.) Then say:

(PSALM 95)

O come, let us sing to the Lord: come, let us every one
A joyful noise make to the Rock of our salvation.
Let us before his presence come
with praise and thankful voice;
Let us sing psalms to him with grace,
and make a joyful noise.
For God, a great God, and great King,
above all gods he is.
Depths of the earth are in his hand,
the strength of hills is his.
To him the spacious sea belongs,
for he the same did make:
The dry land also from his hands
its form at first did take.
O come, and let us worship him,
let us bow down withal,
and on our knees before our Lord the Maker let us fall.
For he's our God, the people we of his own pasture are,
and of his hand the sheep;
to-day, if ye his voice will hear.
Then harden not your hearts, as in the provocation.
As in the desert, on the day of the temptation:
When me your fathers tempt'd and prov'd,
and did my working see;
Ev'n for the space of forty years this race hath grieved me.
I said, this people errs in heart,

my ways they do not know:
To whom I sware in wrath,
that to my rest they should not go.

Sit for ten minutes picturing complete success for the petitioner.

Extinguish the candles.

This should first be done on a Tuesday. Repeat the ritual on Friday, but then light orange candles 1 and 2. The following Tuesday do the ritual again lighting orange candles 1, 2, and 3.

Finally, on the second Friday, do the ritual once more. This time light all four of the orange candles.

If it is felt necessary to do the ceremony over a longer period of time, it may be repeated every Tuesday and Friday from then onward but, after the initial "buildup," always light all candles. Continue until successfully attained.

TRUTH

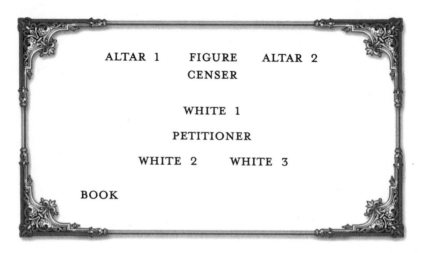

```
        ALTAR  1      FIGURE      ALTAR  2
                      CENSER

                      WHITE  1

                    PETITIONER

            WHITE  2        WHITE  3

    BOOK
```

To Learn the Truth

Light altar candles 1 and 2.

Light incense.

Concentrate on the subject about which you wish to learn the truth.

Light petitioner's candle, thinking about petitioner.

Light white candle 1 and say:

(PSALM 117)

O give ye praise unto the Lord,
all nations that be;
Likewise, ye people all, accord his name to magnify.
For great to us-ward ever are his loving-kindnesses:
His truth endures for evermore.
The Lord O do ye bless.

Light white candle 2 and say:

O give ye praise unto the Lord,
all nations that be;
Likewise, ye people all, accord his name to magnify.
For great to us-ward ever are his loving-kindnesses:
His truth endures for evermore.
The Lord O do ye bless.

Light white candle 3 and say:

O give ye praise unto the Lord,
all nations that be;
Likewise, ye people all, accord his name to magnify.
For great to us-ward ever are his loving-kindnesses:
His truth endures for evermore.
The Lord O do ye bless.

Sit for a half hour in quiet contemplation before extinguishing the candles.

UNCROSSING

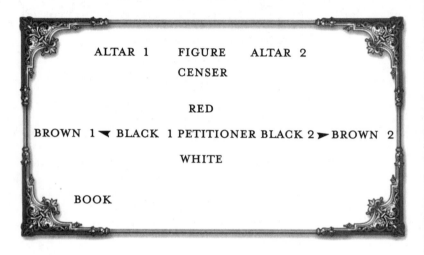

```
          ALTAR 1      FIGURE      ALTAR 2
                       CENSER


                        RED

BROWN 1 ◄ BLACK 1 PETITIONER BLACK 2 ► BROWN 2

                       WHITE


          BOOK
```

To Uncross a Person

Light altar candles 1 and 2.

Light incense.

Light petitioner's candle, thinking of petitioner.

Light red and white candles, thinking of the strength and purity of the petitioner that will help dispel the "crossed" condition.

Light black candles 1 and 2, thinking of the "crossing" of the petitioner, or thinking of the person who crossed the petitioner (if known).

Light brown candles 1 and 2, thinking of the failing and uncertainty of the person who crossed the petitioner. Say:

(PSALM 59)

My God, deliver me from those that are mine enemies;
And do thou me defend from those that up against me rise.
Do thou deliver me from them that work iniquity;
And give me safety from the men of bloody cruelty.
For, lo, they for my soul lay wait: the mighty do combine
Against me, Lord; not for my fault, nor any sin of mine.
They run, and, without any fault in me,
themselves do ready make:
Awake to meet me with thy help; and do thou notice take.
Awake therefore, Lord God of hosts, thou God of Israel,
to visit heathen all: spare none that wickedly rebel.
At ev'ning they go to and fro;
they make great noise and sound,
Like a dog, and often walk about the city round.
Behold, they belch out with their mouth,
and in their lips are swords:
For they do say thus, who is he that now doth hear our words?
But thou, O Lord, shalt laugh at them,
and all the heathen mock.
While he's in power I'll wait on thee;

for God is my high rock.
He of my mercy that is God betimes shall me prevent:
Upon mine en'mies God shall let me see mine heart's content.
Them slay not, lest my folk forget;
but scatter them abroad
By thy strong pow'r; and bring them down,
O thou our shield and God.
For their mouth's sin, and for the words
that from their lips do fly,
let them be taken in their pride;
because they curse and lie.
In wrath consume them, then consume,
that so they may not be:
And that in Jacob God doth rule to the earth's ends let them see.
At ev'ning let thou them return,
making great noise and sound,
Like to a dog, and often walk about the city round.
And let them wander up and down, in seeking food to eat;
And let them grudge when they shall not be satisfy'd with meat.
But of thy pow'r I'll sing aloud; at morn thy mercy praise:
For thou to me my refuge wast, and tow'r, in troublous days.
O God, thou art my strength, I will sing praises unto thee;
For God is my defence, a God of mercy unto me.

Extinguish black and brown candles, then sit for five minutes before extinguishing the others.

Repeat the ritual every three days, each time moving the two black candles outward toward the brown by one or two inches. Continue until the blacks touch the browns.

—⚜ UNDERSTANDING ⚜—

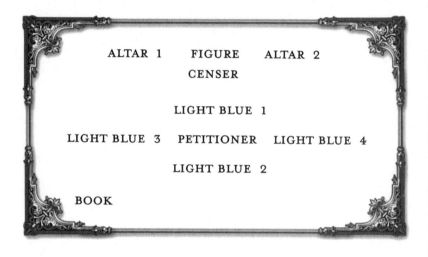

ALTAR 1   FIGURE   ALTAR 2

CENSER

LIGHT BLUE 1

LIGHT BLUE 3   PETITIONER   LIGHT BLUE 4

LIGHT BLUE 2

BOOK

To Develop Understanding

Light altar candles 1 and 2.

Light incense.

Light petitioner's candle while thinking of petitioner.

Light light blue candles 1, 2, 3, and 4.

Think, for a moment, of being understanding; of seeing the other person's point of view; of being sympathetic. Then say:

(PSALM 133)

Behold, how good a thing it is,
and how becoming well,
Together such as brethren are in unity to dwell!
Like precious ointment on the head,
that down the beard did flow,
Ev'n Aaron's beard, and to the skirts did of his garments go.
As Hermon's dew, the dew that doth on Sion's hills descend:
For there the blessing God commands, life that shall never end.

Pause a moment, then repeat:

Behold, how good a thing it is,
and how becoming well,
Together such as brethren are in unity to dwell!
Like precious ointment on the head,
that down the beard did flow,
Ev'n Aaron's beard, and to the skirts did of his garments go.
As Hermon's dew, the dew that doth on Sion's hills descend:
For there the blessing God commands, life that shall never end.

Pause again, then repeat:

Behold, how good a thing it is,
and how becoming well,
Together such as brethren are in unity to dwell!
Like precious ointment on the head,
that down the beard did flow,
Ev'n Aaron's beard, and to the skirts did of his garments go.
As Hermon's dew, the dew that doth on Sion's hills descend:
For there the blessing God commands, life that shall never end.

Sit for a few moments in quiet contemplation before extinguishing the flames. Repeat every night for seven nights.

APPENDIX I

The Darker Side

Any talk of candleburning is invariably, in the "popular mind," associated with the so-called voodoo practice of sticking pins into a wax figure (actually this is not specifically a voodoo practice. It is purely an act of Black Magic). Wax *may* be stuck—and candles burned—for evil purposes, but it is a very dangerous practice, one that can very easily backfire on the practitioner. It may help to describe this particular ritual.

The practitioner takes a piece of wax, or clay, and proceeds to work it, forming it into the general shape of a human being. All the time the practitioner is working, the practitioner keeps his or her mind firmly on the intended victim. The figure may be basically very crude in shape, with no facial or body details—just a body, head, two arms, and two legs—but the practitioner sees it as representing the victim. He sees the victim's face on the figure. He sees the details of his body, his stance, his gestures. To him it *is* the victim.

If there is anything belonging to the victim that can be mixed into the wax, it will help tremendously with the *identification*. Traditionally, nail parings, hair clippings, or the like are worked in. These create a tremendous bond between figure and victim.

When completed, the figure must be named—a parody of baptism. It is sprinkled with salted water and then held in the smoke of incense while the practitioner names it for the intended victim. When that has been done it may be wrapped in a clean white cloth and put on one side until needed.

To actually work the malefic magic, the practitioner takes nine new, unused pins. He lays the wax effigy before him and, taking the pins one at a time, jabs them into the figure with the wish that a particular thing shall happen. For example, he may jab the pins into the figure's head with the words, "May . . . (name) . . . be driven insane!" Or he may stab the figure in the chest, with the words, "May . . . (name) . . . have a heart attack!" For this *sympathetic* magic to work, the practitioner must be really worked up, really angry—must feel so incensed against his or her intended victim that if he or she were present in person, the practitioner, would certainly attack physically.

The big precaution that must be taken by the practitioner is in his or her handling of the pins. As the practitioner thrusts in each one, he or she must be extremely careful not to touch any of the other pins already pushed in. Should the practitioner accidentally brush against even one of them, then *the whole curse* (for that is precisely what it is) *will come back on the practitioner!*

It is interesting to find a custom still very much alive in parts of Britain that involves sticking pins into a candle. Traditionally, if a young woman has been jilted, she should take a candle—it need not be black— and light it. Sitting before it, she should stick two new pins into it, from opposite sides. They should go in far enough to reach the wick. She then recites:

"'Tis not these pins I wish to burn, but . . . (name). . . 's heart I wish to turn. May he neither sleep nor rest 'till he hath granted my request."

She must then sit and watch the candle burn down to the pins, all the time thinking of her lover.

It is possible to purchase special figure candles— usually a red-wax female and black-wax male—from certain suppliers. These are candles in crude human form, with a regular wick running through them. They can be used as in the above-described Black ritual. Since such a candle is already formed, then it must have some object belonging to the victim attached to it, to personalize it. It must also, of course, be sprinkled, censed, and named.

When the pins have been stuck into such a figure-candle and the curse is complete, the practitioner may light the wick and let the candle burn completely down. In this way, the curse is absolutely irrevocable.

The "Hand of Glory" is occasionally mentioned in writings on Black Magic and Sorcery. This hand was, in effect, a form of candelabra. It was actually a hand cut from a dead man, hanging from a gibbet. This gruesome object would be set upright, usually on a chimney-mantel, and five candles set on the tips of the fingers and thumb. The candles were invariably black.

According to an eighteenth-century work*,

The use of the Hand of Glory is to stupefy those to whom it is displayed and render them motionless, in such a way that they can no more stir than if they were dead. It is thus prepared: Take the right or left hand of a felon who is hanging from a gibbet beside a highway; wrap it in part of a funeral pall and so wrapped squeeze it well. Then put it into an earthenware vessel with zimat, nitre, salt and long peppers, the whole well powdered. Leave it in this vessel for two weeks, then take it out and expose it to full sunlight during the dog-days (August, September and October) until it becomes quite dry. If the sun is not strong enough, put it in an oven heated with fern and vervain. Next make a kind of candle with the fat of a gibbeted felon, virgin wax, sesame, and ponie, and use the Hand of Glory as a candlestick . . . then those in every place into which you go with this baneful instrument shall remain motionless.

* *Secrets merveilleux de la magie naturelle et cabalistique du Petit Albert* (1722).

Henri Gamache claims to have found examples of a more modern version of the Hand of Glory. In *The Master Key to Occult Secrets* he says:

> About two pounds of molding clay are obtained and this is formed into the shape of a human hand. A few strands of hair, pieces of cloth taken from the clothes of the enemy or adversary or the person over whom one wishes to hold sway, is mixed with the clay. A socket is molded in the palm of the hand large enough to hold a candle.
>
> Then a black candle is obtained and dressed with oil. This can be the kind of oil called "confusion oil" or "essence of bend over." The oil is rubbed on the candle while saying: "With this oil, I thee control." The operator concentrates on the person who is the subject of the ritual. The candle is inserted in the socket and burned a few minutes each midnight for seven nights.

None of the above malefic forms of magic are recommended. Not only can they be dangerous in themselves—as with the necessarily careful placing of the pins—but they may well be reflected back on the operator, in greatly magnified form, by the intended victim, should he or she have the knowledge (this he or she could do through the use of a "Witch's Bottle" or the like). Do not, therefore, ever attempt to "play" with magic. For magic is a very real power and should be treated with great respect.

APPENDIX II

Over the years since this book first appeared, I have received a number of letters from people, who, through circumstances of living, are unable to burn candles or incense and/or are unable to chant. Some live with parents, relatives, or roommates who would not understand. Some have inquisitive neighbors. One lady says that she lives with a number of cats who would be bound to disturb any arrangement of candles. They all say the same thing: "What can I do? Is there any simple, yet effective magick that can be worked without the use of these tools?"

There *is* a magickal practice that fills the bill and it is closely related to candleburning. It can be extremely effective and can be done virtually anywhere at any time. It is creative visualization.

We can all visualize. When you are stuck in the office but wish you were out on the golf course, you can close your eyes and *see* the golf course with its smooth greens, roughs, sand traps and all. It is not difficult to visualize. When you are thirsty and long for a nice cold beer (soda, or whatever), you can close your eyes and see that beer. In fact the "see-ing" of it—the visualization—creates more of a long-ing and drives you on to the goal of obtaining the beer. So why not let that visualization work for you? Let it create that which you most desire.

Does this mean that if you want to win a million dollars in a lottery, you can just close your eyes and see it, then it's yours? No, of course not. As with all magick (and most other things in life) there are cer-tain rules; certain paths that must be followed if you are to arrive at your destination. The first of these is to set a *REALISTIC GOAL.*

I once lived near two brothers, Eugene and Carl-son. They were as different as could be in all things and served as excellent examples, both of how to go about getting what you want and how not to go about getting what you want, by whatever means. Take jobs, for example. When they left school, both boys wanted good-paying jobs. Carlson declared that he would never settle for a low-paying job . . . he was going to live the good life! Eugene didn't say much but went out and got a job as a bag-packer at the local super-market. It paid very little, but it was something.

As the months wore on, Carlson kept on looking for a job that was not "beneath him." Meanwhile, Eugene was promoted to working the cash register and from there later progressed to assistant manager.

Carlson not only wanted a fine job, he also wanted a new, expensive, car. While he kept search-ing—and growing more bitter—Eugene bought himself an old secondhand Volkswagen. After he had been working for a while, and had saved a little money, he traded it in for a better secondhand car.

Eventually, of course, Carlson had to break down and take what job he could get. He remained bitter. By that time Eugene was a store manager and owned a brand-new car.

This slice of life is a good example of setting realis-tic goals. Carison's goal—to "start at the top," with a top job and a new car—was unrealistic. Eugene's—working up, a step at a time—was realistic. Now the same type of advancement holds true in creative visu-alization. You cannot conjure up a brand-new Cadil-lac but, if the need exists for a car, you can certainly conjure up a secondhand vehicle and go on from there.

Does this mean you can never get a brand-new car through creative visualization? No. It simply means that, with some things, you may have to take several steps to get there rather than just one. If a new Cadillac is your goal in life—the one thing above all others that you feel you must have—then it is going to take a number of steps to get it. Like Eugene, you should start out with a secondhand car. Know that it is only a step in the direction you wish to go. Know that that car will soon give way to another, better, secondhand vehicle and that, in turn, perhaps to a third. But know also that these step-goals are all leading to the final, ultimate goal . . . where you will eventually be trading in your last secondhand car and getting that new Cadillac.

So when your ultimate goal seems far distant, set step-goals. Plan them out. How many steps, *realistically,* do you think it will take to get to where you want to be? Put it down on paper and decide, then you'll know in which direction you are heading and how long it may take to get there.

Along with a realistic goal you must also set a *REALISTIC TIME LIMIT.* Your car—whether new or old —will not appear in your driveway overnight. Creative visualization is not a magick wand to be waved for instant magick. Like all magick, you have to work at it, so decide for how long you are going to work. Generally speaking, a month is a good length of time. In fact, as you will see below, it can help to tiein your creative visualization with the phases of the moon. Not everything can be accomplished in one month, of course, but think in terms of lunar units . . . one month; two months; three months.

To get that first secondhand car, one month is a *reasonable amount of time.* When you've got the car and have enjoyed it for awhile, then you can start thinking about the trade up. A better car will take a little longer, so when you're ready to start, allow *two* months on that one, and so on with each step up towards that final goal.

The important move now is to work out your program on paper. What are your goals . . . the ultimate, and, if necessary, the step-goals? What are the time limits? Here is the place to really consider the form your goal will take. With something like a car, it's fairly distinct. But take a goal like a "better job." What sort of job? In what way "better"? More pay? Less work? More pleasant surroundings? *Be very specific.* Write it all down, so that it's not just a fuzzy, vague idea in the back of your mind. You want to move from that lousy apartment into a house? What sort of house? A baronial mansion, or an unpretentious little cottage? (Remember to start small.) Let there be no ambiguity. Write down all the details, and if necessary, draw a picture.

Pictures can be great aids for creative visualization. Again, you can use the example of a new car— on the wall of your room hang a photograph of the specific car you want. Look at it often. Be able to see it at any time, with your eyes closed. See it and know that *it is your car.* The same with anything else you are working toward. If you can't have a picture, hang up a word or sentence, *"PLEASANT WORKING CONDITIONS WITH FRIENDLY CO-WORKERS"* . . . *"SMILE"* . . . *"SUEDE LEATHER JACKET"*. . . write it in bold letters and hang it on the wall of your room,

or around the mirror on your dressing table. See it
and keep seeing it.

To return, for a moment, to the question of
whether or not the goal is realistic—are you sure
you really do *want* whatever it is? If you want a
house rather than the apartment . . . can you afford
to keep a house? Have you considered the atten-
dant maintenance, taxes, utilities, etc., that go with
a house and not necessarily with an apartment?
That car you want . . . will you be able to afford to
run it when you've got it? Have you considered the
rising price of gas, the insurance, taxes, etc.?

As you see, there are many things to consider
when you are wishing for change. But once you've
considered all the pros and cons and have made up
your mind . . . *think positively.* Get your goal clear in
your mind and then go for it! It is going to require
hard work and dedication; it is going to require
patience. But it can be done.

So much for the general details: Now for the
mechanics of the process. When do you do your
creative visualization? How? And where?

You can really do it anywhere but, for best results,
I would recommend much the same thing that I
suggested for candleburning. Let it be somewhere
that is quiet; where you don't hear the stereo or the
television. In your bedroom is probably the best
place. Make sure that you will remain undisturbed
for the twenty minutes or so you will be working.

Dress comfortably (or don't dress at all). You can either sit in a chair or lie on your bed.

If you sit in a chair, let it be one with good back support and—most important—one that allows you to sit with your back straight. Whether sitting or lying, the important thing is to have your spine as straight as possible. The chair may have arms on which you can rest your arms. If it does not have arms then let your hands rest lightly in your lap.

The morning or early evening is possibly the best time to do your visualization. Late evening is not good since you will be tired and may just fall asleep, so do it when you feel rested. And try to do it at the same time every day.

If you are in a situation where you can burn incense, then burn a little while you work at this. Any pleasant-smelling incense will do, though a combination of frankincense, cinnamon, and mastic is a great aid to concentration.

Relax your body and start off with some heavy breathing. Try the following exercise:

Allow the head to tip fully backwards.

Breathe deeply in and out three times.

Return to the upright position.

Tip the head as far as possible to the left.

Breathe deeply in and out three times.

Return to the upright position. Tip the head as far as possible to the right. Breathe deeply in and out three times. Return to the upright position.

Allow the head to fall forward then move it in a circle, counterclockwise, three times.

Repeat the last exercise, moving the head clockwise three times.

Return to the upright position.

Breathe in through the nose with a number of short, sharp, intakes until the lungs are full. Hold it a moment, then suddenly exhale through the mouth with a "Hah!" sound. Do this three times.

Breathe in slowly and fully, through the right nostril (if necessary, hold the left one closed). Hold it a moment then exhale slowly through the mouth. Do this three times then repeat, breathing in through the left nostril and out through the right nostril.

Now feel your body relaxing and, breathing normally but deeply, concentrate your thoughts till you can imagine your whole body encased in a ball of white light. This is the white light of purity and of protection.

Never start any psychic exercise without first placing yourself within this light.

Now, to finish calming your body and to "center" you, chant a short psalm. If you are able to do this aloud, do so. If not (through close proximity of roommates) then say it quietly to yourself. You can either say the Christian Twenty-third Psalm or the Pagan Seax-Wica Psalm*, which is as follows: —

*Ever as I pass through the ways
do I feel the presence of the gods.
I know that in aught I do
They are with me
and I with them,
forever.
No evil shall be entertained,
for purity is the dweller
within me and about me.
For good do I strive
and for good do I live.
Love unto all things.
So be it, forever.*

I have mentioned working with the moons. Start your work immediately following the full moon. You are going to be working at it for one lunar month (twenty-eight days) so, although you will be starting off in the waning cycle, you will be doing your best work—and working up to the climax—in the waxing cycle, culminating at the next full moon. That is as it should be.

You are now ready to start your creative visualization. You are relaxed. You are protected. You have a clear goal in mind and know that it can be achieved.

* Copyright Raymond Buckland, 1981.

Close your eyes and see your objective in your mind's eye. See it and *know* that *it is yours.* Do not see it and just wish that it were yours, or see it on the way to being yours. See it and *know* that it is yours. If it's a car, see yourself driving it. See it in your garage. See yourself polishing it and filling it with gas. See yourself putting the keys in your pocket.

If it's a job, see yourself working at the job. Not just getting it, but already there and working. If it's a promotion, see yourself in the new position. We create our own reality so do it in the most positive sense. Create it by seeing, always, the end result—the goal achieved.

Keep up this visualization for at least ten minutes. Afterward, relax. Gradually bring yourself back to your surroundings, slowly dissipating the sphere of white light about you. You will afterward feel refreshed; not depleted.

Do your creative visualization every day. Think positively and have patience. You will gain your goals.

Raymond Buckland came to the United States from England in 1962. In the past thirty years he has had over thirty books published—fiction and nonfiction—by such publishers as Ace Books, Warner Books, Prentice Hall, Samuel Weiser, Inner Traditions International, Galde Press, Citadel, Visible Ink Press, and Llewellyn Worldwide, Ltd., with more than a million copies in print and translations in sixteen foreign languages. He has also written newspaper and magazine articles and five screenplays. He has twice won the Coalition of Visionary Retailer's Visionary Award.

Considered an authority on the occult and the supernatural, he has lectured at colleges and universities across the country and has been the subject of articles in such newspapers and magazines as *The New York Times, Los Angeles Times, New York Daily* (and Sunday) *News,* Cosmopolitan, and many others.

Raymond Buckland has appeared on numerous radio and television talk programs, including *The Dick Cavett Show, Tom Snyder's Tomorrow Show,* and *Not For Women Only* (with Barbara Walters). He has taught courses at several universities, including New York State University and Hofstra University. Today he lives on a small farm in north-central Ohio.

Many of Llewellyn's authors have websites with additional information and resources. For more information, please visit our website at www.llewellyn.com.